GOVERNMENT PROCEDURES AND OPERATIONS

FEDERAL REAL PROPERTY

ANALYSES OF KEY ISSUES

GOVERNMENT PROCEDURES AND OPERATIONS

Additional books in this series can be found on Nova's website under the Series tab.

Additional e-books in this series can be found on Nova's website under the e-book tab.

GOVERNMENT PROCEDURES AND OPERATIONS

FEDERAL REAL PROPERTY

ANALYSES OF KEY ISSUES

ADAM B. CLARK
EDITOR

nova publishers
New York

Library of Congress Cataloging-in-Publication Data

ISBN: 978-1-63482-278-7

Published by Nova Science Publishers, Inc. † New York

CONTENTS

Preface		**vii**
Chapter 1	Authorization of General Services Administration Real Property Projects: Current Process and Proposed Legislation *Garrett Hatch*	**1**
Chapter 2	Capital Financing: Alternative Approaches to Budgeting for Federal Real Property *United States Government Accountability Office*	**17**
Chapter 3	Overseas Real Property: State Department Needs to Improve Guidance and Records Management *United States Government Accountability Office*	**59**
Chapter 4	Overview of Federal Real Property Disposal Requirements and Procedures *Garrett Hatch, Daniel H. Else, Linda Luther, David M. Bearden and Kristina Alexander*	**89**
Index		**117**

PREFACE

Prior to seeking appropriations, The General Services Administration (GSA)is required to obtain congressional authorization for constructing, purchasing, leasing, or renovating real property. The GSA controls more than 8,700 owned and leased buildings with 422 million square feet of floor space, which represents about 12.6% of the government's 3.354 billion total building square footage. GSA has the authority to acquire, operate, and dispose of real property on behalf of other federal agencies, including the judiciary. Its portfolio includes courthouses, land ports of entry, and federal office space. This book provides an analyses of key issues of federal real property.

Chapter 1 - The General Services Administration (GSA) controls more than 8,700 owned and leased buildings with 422 million square feet of floor space, which represents about 12.6% of the government's 3.354 billion total building square footage .Sometimes referred to as the "government's landlord," GSA has the authority to acquire, operate, and dispose of real property on behalf of other federal agencies, including the judiciary. Its portfolio includes courthouses, land ports of entry, and federal office space.

Prior to seeking appropriations, GSA is required to obtain congressional authorization for constructing, purchasing, leasing, or renovating real property. To that end, GSA submits a prospectus to two committees—the Senate Committee on Environment and Public Works and the House Committee on Transportation and Infrastructure—for each proposal that exceeds $2.85 million. The prospectus provides detailed information about the project, including its location and estimated cost. By law, a project that exceeds the $2.85 million threshold may not receive appropriations unless both committees pass resolutions approving of the prospectus.

While the prospectus process provides Congress an opportunity to evaluate GSA real property activities, oversight may be limited by data that are not available to the authorizing committees. GSA's prospectuses, for example, do not always include a comparison of the costs of leasing versus owning space over time, which means Congress is making decisions without knowing whether a proposed project is the most cost effective option. Similarly, many lease prospectuses do not include the cost of altering space to meet agency needs, such as upgraded security, which means authorizing committees may not be aware of the full costs of the projects they are considering. In addition, there are instances where GSA fails to submit prospectuses for projects that exceed the threshold.

Several bills in the 113th Congress propose reforms to the real property process, particularly the process for disposing of unneeded buildings. Examples include the Excess Federal Building and Property Disposal Act (H.R. 328), the Federal Real Property Asset Management Reform Act (S. 1398), and the Civilian Property Realignment Act (H.R. 695 and S. 1715). Another bill, the Public Building Service Savings and Reform Act of 2013 (H.R. 2612) proposes changing the prospectus approval process. The bill would require GSA to include in its prospectuses a plan to offset any new space acquired by eliminating an equal amount of existing space from its inventory. It would also require GSA to ensure it is obtaining the best possible rental rate for leases that fall below the prospectus threshold. Other provisions would require GSA to provide the authorizing committees with an annual report listing all of the leases it entered into during the previous fiscal year; to notify Congress if a project's costs increased by 5% or more; and, when requesting authorization to acquire space, to explain why existing federal space could not be used.

H.R. 2612 could mitigate several long-standing weaknesses in the prospectus process. The bill proposes to help control costs by ensuring that the authorizing committees have access to comparative cost data, and by requiring GSA to provide cost estimates of alterations associated with a new lease that are not included in the estimate of rent. In addition, H.R. 2612 might enhance oversight by requiring GSA to provide a more detailed justification for requesting new space, and to notify Congress when a project exceeds the cost and size parameters established in the prospectus.

Chapter 2 - Federal real property projects are fully funded when Congress provides budget authority and appropriations for the estimated full cost of the projects up front—at the time they are undertaken. However, as agencies work to balance limited resources with mission demands, many have turned to approaches other than full upfront funding to acquire, renovate, or dispose of federal real property, such as buildings, structures, and land. GAO was asked to review alternative models for managing federal real property. This report examines (1) agency experiences funding federal real property projects, (2) some of the alternative funding mechanisms selected agencies use, as well as agency experiences using selected mechanisms, and (3) alternative budgetary structures within the current unified budget that may potentially help Congress and agencies better recognize the cost of real property projects and associated returns, promoting both transparency and fiscal control. GAO reviewed case study projects from 4 agencies among the top 10 in federal real property holdings and chosen based on their use of alternative funding mechanisms, as identified in their past and ongoing work. Finally, GAO identified alternative budgetary structures that may support real property projects and principles for considering them by reviewing published reports and interviewing federal budget staff and experts.

GAO is not making any recommendations in this report. GSA, USDA, VA, and Interior generally agreed with their findings. USDA, Interior and VA provided technical comments that were incorporated as appropriate.

Chapter 3 - The Department of State (State) holds or leases about 70-million square feet of real estate in about 275 posts worldwide and has the authority to construct, acquire, manage, and dispose of real property abroad.

GAO was asked to review State's management of overseas real property. This report examines: (1) what is known about State's overseas real property inventory, and (2) what factors State considers in managing its overseas real property portfolio and to what extent it documents its decision-making process pertaining to real property.

GAO requested 202 files for all acquisitions, disposals, and major leases pertaining to State's management of its real property abroad for the period from 2008-2013. In addition, GAO interviewed State officials in headquarters and at four posts abroad, selected because they had (1) ongoing or recently completed embassy construction or renovation projects without property disposals, (2) properties reported as identified for disposal for multiple years without being disposed, and (3) both owned and leased properties. The results of the four case studies cannot be generalized for the purpose of this review.

Chapter 4 - The federal government holds thousands of properties that agencies no longer need to accomplish their missions. When the government disposes of unneeded properties—through transfer, donation, or sale—it generates savings by eliminating maintenance costs. In addition, when state or local governments, nonprofits, or businesses acquire unneeded federal properties, they may be used to provide services to the public, such as temporary housing, or contribute to economic development.

The General Services Administration (GSA) plays a central role in disposing of unneeded property at most federal agencies. The Federal Real Property and Administrative Services Act of 1949 (Property Act) gives GSA the authority to dispose of real property at all federal agencies unless they have independent statutory authority to dispose of their own properties themselves. A number of agencies have independent disposal authority—ranging from limited to broad in scope—including two of the largest federal landholders, the U.S. Postal Service (USPS) and the Department of Defense.

When an agency notifies GSA that it has unneeded real property, GSA first offers to transfer the property to another federal agency, which must pay fair market value for it. If no other agency wishes to acquire the property, GSA may then convey it to a state or local government, or a qualified nonprofit, for up to a 100% discount—provided it is used for an approved public benefit. Should a state or local government or qualified nonprofit wish to acquire the property for a use other than one of the approved public benefits, GSA has the option to sell the property to them at fair market value. Finally, if the property is not sold to a public or nonprofit entity, it is offered for sale to the public.

The disposal of a federal property may be subject to a number of environmental requirements and historic preservation mandates, although which requirements apply depends on a number of site-specific conditions. Three principal federal statutes govern the environmental review process, identification and remediation of hazardous substances, and historic preservation: the National Environmental Protection Act (NEPA), the Comprehensive Environmental Response, Compensation and Liability Act of 1980 (CERCLA), and the National Historic Preservation Act (NHPA).

Among the agencies with independent statutory disposal authority, USPS has the greatest autonomy. The Postal Service has, in essence, been granted the authority to dispose of its properties as it deems appropriate, without the assistance of GSA. DOD also has independent statutory disposal authority, but of a more limited scope. DOD must use GSA to dispose of all properties that do not otherwise fall under the scope of special, temporary disposal authorities, commonly referred to as Base Realignment and Closure (BRAC) legislation.

In: Federal Real Property: Analyses of Key Issues ISBN: 978-1-63482-278-7
Editor: Adam B. Clark

Chapter 1

AUTHORIZATION OF GENERAL SERVICES ADMINISTRATION REAL PROPERTY PROJECTS: CURRENT PROCESS AND PROPOSED LEGISLATION*

Garrett Hatch

SUMMARY

The General Services Administration (GSA) controls more than 8,700 owned and leased buildings with 422 million square feet of floor space, which represents about 12.6% of the government's 3.354 billion total building square footage .Sometimes referred to as the "government's landlord," GSA has the authority to acquire, operate, and dispose of real property on behalf of other federal agencies, including the judiciary. Its portfolio includes courthouses, land ports of entry, and federal office space.

Prior to seeking appropriations, GSA is required to obtain congressional authorization for constructing, purchasing, leasing, or renovating real property. To that end, GSA submits a prospectus to two committees—the Senate Committee on Environment and Public Works and the House Committee on Transportation and Infrastructure—for each

* This is an edited, reformatted and augmented version of a Congressional Research Service publication R43443, prepared for Members and Committees of Congress, dated March 27, 2014.

proposal that exceeds $2.85 million. The prospectus provides detailed information about the project, including its location and estimated cost. By law, a project that exceeds the $2.85 million threshold may not receive appropriations unless both committees pass resolutions approving of the prospectus.

While the prospectus process provides Congress an opportunity to evaluate GSA real property activities, oversight may be limited by data that are not available to the authorizing committees. GSA's prospectuses, for example, do not always include a comparison of the costs of leasing versus owning space over time, which means Congress is making decisions without knowing whether a proposed project is the most cost effective option. Similarly, many lease prospectuses do not include the cost of altering space to meet agency needs, such as upgraded security, which means authorizing committees may not be aware of the full costs of the projects they are considering. In addition, there are instances where GSA fails to submit prospectuses for projects that exceed the threshold.

Several bills in the 113th Congress propose reforms to the real property process, particularly the process for disposing of unneeded buildings. Examples include the Excess Federal Building and Property Disposal Act (H.R. 328), the Federal Real Property Asset Management Reform Act (S. 1398), and the Civilian Property Realignment Act (H.R. 695 and S. 1715). Another bill, the Public Building Service Savings and Reform Act of 2013 (H.R. 2612) proposes changing the prospectus approval process. The bill would require GSA to include in its prospectuses a plan to offset any new space acquired by eliminating an equal amount of existing space from its inventory. It would also require GSA to ensure it is obtaining the best possible rental rate for leases that fall below the prospectus threshold. Other provisions would require GSA to provide the authorizing committees with an annual report listing all of the leases it entered into during the previous fiscal year; to notify Congress if a project's costs increased by 5% or more; and, when requesting authorization to acquire space, to explain why existing federal space could not be used.

H.R. 2612 could mitigate several long-standing weaknesses in the prospectus process. The bill proposes to help control costs by ensuring that the authorizing committees have access to comparative cost data, and by requiring GSA to provide cost estimates of alterations associated with a new lease that are not included in the estimate of rent. In addition, H.R. 2612 might enhance oversight by requiring GSA to provide a more detailed justification for requesting new space, and to notify Congress when a project exceeds the cost and size parameters established in the prospectus.

THE GOVERNMENT'S LANDLORD

The General Services Administration (GSA) is the federal government's primary civilian real property management agency with 11 regional offices that oversee GSA owned and leased properties across the nation. At the end of FY2012, GSA—through its real property office, the Public Buildings Service (PBS)—owned or leased 8,708 buildings with more than 422 million square feet of floor space, which represents about 12.6% of the government's 3.354 billion total building square footage.[1] GSA's inventory includes offices, courthouses, and land ports of entry.[2] Given the breadth of GSA's holdings, the agency is sometimes referred to as "the government's landlord."

Until Congress enacted the Public Buildings Act in 1926, construction authority for each federal building was approved and funded in separate pieces of legislation.[3] The 1926 act provided the basic authority for the construction of federal buildings through the congressional authorization and appropriation process. Congress later enacted the Public Buildings Act of 1949 to authorize the planning, site acquisition, and design of federal buildings located outside of Washington, DC, and for improvements to existing federal buildings.[4] Congress also enacted the Federal Property and Administrative Services Act of 1949, which established the General Services Administration (GSA), and gave the GSA Administrator (Administrator) responsibility for administering federal real property.[5] In 1954, Congress amended the Public Buildings Act of 1949 to authorize the Administrator to acquire titles to real property and to construct federal buildings through lease-purchase contracts. Under this procedure, a building was financed by private capital, and the federal government made installment payments on the purchase price in lieu of rent payments. Title to the property was vested in the federal government at the end of the contract period, which could range from 10 to 30 years. When authority for lease-purchase contracts expired in 1957, Congress approved a successor statute, the Public Buildings Act of 1959.[6] The 1959 act reestablished earlier requirements to provide for direct federal construction of public buildings through the congressional authorization and appropriation process. This act, as amended and re-codified over the years, remains the basic statute authorizing the Administrator to construct, own, lease, operate, maintain, and renovate buildings to serve civilian agencies of the federal government.[7] Notably, while GSA works with many executive branch agencies and the judiciary to meet their space needs, it generally does not perform real property functions on behalf of the legislative branch.

GSA is responsible for the design and construction of its buildings and courthouses, and for repairs and alterations to existing facilities, including those that are leased. As part of the President's annual budget submission to Congress, GSA requests funding for new construction projects, as well as for purchasing, renovating, and leasing existing properties. Congress authorizes appropriations for these projects, however, through the prospectus approval process, which is discussed below.

PROSPECTUS APPROVAL PROCESS

Under the Public Buildings Act, as amended (PBA), GSA is required to submit a formal document, known as a prospectus, to the Senate Committee on Environment and Public Works and the House Committee on Transportation and Infrastructure (referred to throughout this report as the authorizing committees) as part of the process to authorize and appropriate funds for constructing, purchasing, leasing, or renovating real property.[8] Each prospectus must include

- a brief description of the building to be constructed, altered, or leased;
- the building's location;
- an estimate of the maximum cost of the project;
- a statement by the Administrator that suitable space in existing government-owned buildings is not available;
- a statement of rents and other housing costs currently being paid by agencies that would occupy the newly constructed, renovated, or leased space; and
- an estimate of the future energy performance of the building.

A prospectus is only required for projects with estimated costs that meet or exceed a specified amount, referred to as the prospectus threshold. Under authorities provided in 40 U.S.C. § 3307, GSA establishes annual prospectus thresholds for four different types of real property activities. A description of each threshold is provided in *Table 1* below.

Table 1. Dollar Thresholds for Submission of Prospectuses, FY2014

Real Property Activity	Amount	Authority
Construction, alteration, or acquisition of a public building	$2,850,000	40 U.S.C. § 3307(a)(1)
Acquisition of leased space	$2,850,000	40 U.S.C. § 3307(a)(2)
Alteration of leased space	$1,425,000	40 U.S.C. § 3307(a)(3)
Acquisition of leased space specifically to accommodate computer and telecommunications operations; secure or sensitive activities related to national defense and security; and permanent courtrooms, judicial chambers, or administrative offices for any U.S. court	$2,850,000	40 U.S.C. § 3307(g)

Source: Letter from Dan Tangherlini, General Services Administration Acting Administrator, to Senator Barbara Boxer, Chairman, Committee on Environment and Public Works, June 4, 2013.

GSA has the authority to adjust these thresholds each year in order "to reflect a percentage increase or decrease in construction costs during the prior calendar year."[9] GSA adjusts the thresholds based on the Building Cost Index of the *Engineering News-Record*, an industry trade journal published by McGraw-Hill.[10]

As noted, for each project that meets or exceeds the appropriate threshold, GSA must submit a prospectus to the authorizing committees. Each committee must pass a resolution approving the prospectus before the project is authorized to receive appropriations.[11] The resolutions must only be approved at the committee level—floor action is not required. If an appropriation is not made within one year after the date the prospectus was approved, the committees may pass resolutions rescinding their approval.[12]

Congress appropriates funds for GSA's authorized construction and leasing projects each fiscal year through the Financial Services and General Government appropriations bill. Once a proposed project receives congressional funding—and not all authorized projects do—GSA's Public Buildings Service contracts with private sector firms for design and construction work. When leasing space, GSA searches for space that meets energy efficiency and renewable energy performance goals.[13]

In times of emergency or disaster—such as when a hurricane causes structural damage to a federal building—the normal prospectus thresholds and procedures are temporarily lifted to enable GSA to quickly find new space for displaced federal employees. To that end, GSA is authorized to enter into an emergency lease agreement without an approved prospectus during any period "declared by the President to require emergency leasing authority."[14] Emergency leases may not exceed 180 days, however, without an approved prospectus.[15]

It is not uncommon for the cost of real property projects—particularly the construction of new buildings—to escalate as the project proceeds. GSA is required to resubmit an amended prospectus for congressional approval if the cost of the project exceeds the approved estimated maximum amount by more than 10%.[16]

PROSPECTUS APPROVAL AS OVERSIGHT

The prospectus approval process provides Congress with an opportunity to exercise oversight of GSA's real property activities. With a multi-billion dollar budget and thousands of buildings under its control, GSA manages one of the government's largest and most diverse real property portfolios. Moreover, given its role as the procurer of space for numerous other agencies, congressional oversight of GSA's prospectus-level proposals has broad implications. In recent years, for example, GSA has submitted prospectuses to consolidate the headquarters of the Department of Homeland Security at the St. Elizabeth's Campus in Washington, DC; construct a new courthouse in Rockford, IL; and expand a land port of entry in San Diego, CA. These projects illustrate the central role GSA-controlled buildings often play in helping federal agencies fulfill their unique missions. The prospectus process provides an opportunity for Congress to assess how well GSA's proposals meet the needs of its clients and to reject those that it finds poorly conceived or unnecessary.

Congress may also use the prospectus approval process to evaluate cost and space projections. It is not uncommon for GSA to estimate that a single real property project will cost hundreds of millions, or even billions of dollars. Poor project planning may result in cost escalation and unneeded space. The 33 courthouses built between 2000 and 2010, for example, included 3.56 million square feet of unneeded space, which in turn resulted in an additional $835 million in construction expenditures.[17] This prompted Congress to ask the Government Accountability Office (GAO) to audit multiple courthouse construction and renovation projects to identify the origins of widespread cost overruns, and to hold hearings on how to address courthouse cost escalation.[18] At a time when the debt and deficit are salient issues, prospectus approval may be considered an opportunity for Congress to control costs and avoid wasteful spending.

Factors That Limit Oversight

The usefulness of the prospectus approval process as an oversight tool may be limited by data that are not available to authorizing committees. The lack of data that directly compare the cost of leasing versus owning space means that Congress is unable to determine whether it is being asked to approve the most cost-effective option for meeting an agency's real property needs. Similarly, the lack of data on the cost of alterations may prevent Congress from knowing the full costs associated with a particular lease prospectus. Oversight may also be limited by the number of real property projects for which prospectuses should be submitted as required by statute, but are not.

Lack of Comparative Cost Data

One of the primary reasons GAO has listed federal real property management as a high-risk area since 2003 is that the government increasingly acquires space through leases rather than by constructing or purchasing buildings.[19] Since 2008, GSA's portfolio has included more leased than owned space, even though leasing is often less cost effective, particularly if the space will be needed for long-term occupancy (20 years or more).[20] One study of 27 long-term leases estimated that the government will spend $866 million more than it would have spent building or buying comparable space.[21] Nonetheless, GSA's lease prospectuses do not include a comparison of the costs of leasing versus owning space over time, known as an alternative analysis. While GSA is not required by law to include an alternative analysis in its prospectuses, the absence of comparative cost data means Congress is making decisions without knowing whether a proposed lease is the most cost-effective option.

Lack of Data on the Cost of Alterations

The cost of leasing space is more than the sum of rent and operating expenses—in some cases, agencies need to alter leased space in order for it to meet the agencies' needs. An agency may determine, for example, that while the location and square footage are suitable, security features may need to be enhanced, technological capabilities upgraded, or conference rooms added.[22] Such alterations are not necessarily included in the cost estimate of a lease prospectus because the actual building in which space will be leased has not been selected when GSA submits a prospectus. Typically, GSA first seeks authorization to enter into a lease and then identifies suitable space through a competitive process. Moreover, any investment in alterations will be lost if the agency moves to another location at the end of the lease term—a factor that may dissuade the agency relocating, even if a different property was less costly or otherwise more suitable. Alterations to leased space can add millions of dollars to the cost of the lease and affect agency decision-making, but authorizing committees may not know about them and thus not take them into consideration because they are not part of the prospectus.

Failure to Meet Prospectus Submission Requirements

As noted, GSA is required by law to obtain congressional approval if a project exceeds its authorized cost estimate by more than 10%. This approval is obtained by submitting an amended prospectus with the new estimate to the House and Senate authorizing committees. For example, GSA submitted amended prospectuses for courthouse construction projects that exceeded their authorized cost estimates by more than 10%, as required. While the same rule applies to leased space, there is evidence that GSA does not consistently submit amended prospectuses when the cost of a previously authorized lease increased by more than 10%.[23] Similarly, a prospectus must be submitted for leases that initially fell below the prospectus threshold—and therefore did not require congressional authorization—but which were amended so that the new cost of the lease exceeded the threshold. As with leases that increased in cost by more than 10%, auditors have identified multiple instances where GSA did not submit a prospectus for leases that exceeded the prospectus threshold after being amended.[24]

LEGISLATIVE PROPOSAL TO CHANGE THE PROSPECTUS PROCESS

In an effort to make GSA's real property activities more cost effective and transparent, Representative Lou Barletta introduced H.R. 2612, the Public

Buildings Service Savings and Reform Act, on July 8, 2013. The legislation was co-sponsored by Delegate Eleanor Holmes Norton, Representative Bill Shuster, and Representative Nick Rahall. The bill was referred to the Committee on Transportation and Infrastructure, and then on July 9, to the Subcommittee on Economic Development, Public Buildings and Emergency Management. The following day, after committee markup, the committee ordered the bill to be reported; the subcommittee was discharged from further consideration of the bill. No further action has been taken.

The bill would make numerous changes to the way that the Public Buildings Service (PBS)—the office within GSA responsible for real property management—constructs and leases space, reports on the size and cost of GSA's portfolio, and tracks administrative expenses, such as travel and conference costs. The provisions that relate specifically to the prospectus approval process are discussed below.

Key Provisions Related to Prospectus Process

Required Offsets for New Space

Section 2(a) would require any prospectus that proposes new space, whether leased or owned, in fiscal years 2014, 2015, 2016, and 2017, to include the details of the elimination of at least an equal amount of space from GSA's inventory. The following paragraph, 2(b), does not apply to prospectuses but would prohibit GSA from increasing its leased or owned space when compared to its FY2012 inventory as a baseline. Section 2(a) therefore appears to establish a mechanism for Congress to verify that GSA is implementing the offset requirements of Section 2(b).

Restrictions on Below-Prospectus Projects

Section 3(b) would prohibit GSA from entering into a lease that falls below the prospectus threshold but exceeds the "maximum rental rate established by the Administrator for the respective geographical location" unless GSA notifies the authorizing committees in writing at least 10 days before entering into the lease. This provision appears to codify existing GSA policy.[25] In essence, the proposed language would prevent GSA from signing a lease where the rental rate would be greater than that paid for comparable properties in a geographic area. This language would apply specifically to leases that fall below the annual threshold and therefore do not have prospectuses approved by authorizing committees. This may suggest that the provision is intended to prevent GSA from paying above-market rental rates on smaller leases that have less oversight.

Reports on Leases

Section 4(a) would require GSA to submit to the authorizing committees, by December 3 of each year, a list of all leases that it entered into during the previous fiscal year. The list must include, for each lease, its size, location, tenant agency, total annual rent, and authorized annual rent (for prospectus-level leases only).

Zero-Based Space Justification

Section 5(3) would require GSA to include in all prospectuses, whether for construction, purchase, alteration, or lease of space, an explanation of why such space could not be obtained from existing unused space in federal properties.

Eliminating Project Cost Escalation

Section 13 would clarify that a project may not increase or decrease in scope or size by more than 10% unless an amended prospectus is submitted to, and approved by the authorizing committees. It would also require GSA to notify the authorizing committees, in writing, of any project that would increase in cost, or increase or decrease in scope or size beyond its authorized size or scope by 5% or more.

Analysis

If H.R. 2612 is enacted it could result in significant changes in GSA's management of real property, the most sweeping of which might be the offset of space requirements. These requirements, found in Section 2 of the bill, would prohibit GSA from increasing the size of its portfolio above its FY2012 level. Any proposal to build, lease, or purchase new space would have to be offset by an equivalent reduction in existing GSA space, and the details of that offset would have to be included in the project's prospectus. The government owns tens of thousands of properties with unused space—including approximately 11,600 buildings that are less than halfoccupied—and GSA is currently required to first try to fill new space needs at those underutilized federal properties before constructing, purchasing, or leasing space from the private sector.[26]

H.R. 2612 would go further, mandating that GSA actually dispose of—rather than merely consider utilizing—unneeded federal building space as a condition of obtaining new space. The principle of offsetting space is consistent with current legislative proposals to streamline and accelerate the disposal of unneeded federal property.[27] With regard to H.R. 2612, the current disposal process presents a challenge of timing: statutory disposal requirements and local market conditions make it difficult to estimate how long it will take to dispose of a property. Agencies are required by statute, for example, to first offer to transfer unneeded property to other federal agencies that may need it, then offer to convey it to state or local governments and non-profits that might use it for a public benefit, such as a homeless shelter or medical center, and, finally, if the property was neither transferred nor conveyed, offer it for sale to the public.[28] Each step can take weeks—or months—as properties are assessed by interested parties, applications are submitted and reviewed, and financial and legal terms established. Moreover, the condition of the building, the need for the kind of space that is available, and the cost of any required historical or environmental remediation are all local factors that could affect how long it takes to dispose of the property. Some properties may generate no interest at all. It is not clear how H.R. 2612 would take the unpredictable nature of disposition into account. The bill requires "the details of the elimination" of space, but it does not specify whether the space must have already been disposed of prior to the submission of the prospectus, or whether GSA would meet the offsetting requirement by providing a plan for disposing of equivalent space within a given timeframe. It is also not clear how Congress would track proposed disposals to ensure they are completed as detailed in the prospectus. Congress may consider requiring GSA to include in its Performance and Accountability Report or annual budget justification a list of the status of all offset activities approved through the prospectus process.

A related provision of H.R. 2612, the zero-space justification requirement, would also use the prospectus process to constrain the size of GSA's portfolio. By requiring GSA to justify, in its prospectuses, why it must obtain the space requested from a private landholder instead of a federal agency, the provision would increase transparency into GSA's decision-making. Currently, GSA is required to first consider acquiring space in underutilized federal buildings before looking to the private sector to lease or buy space, or to construct new buildings. It is not known how consistently it is undertaken or what criteria are evaluated when determining suitability. The bill does not establish what specific information should be included in the explanation, which could limit the usefulness of the prospectus as an oversight mechanism. GSA could simply state, for example, that there was no suitable space available given the tenant's requirements. Congress may wish to consider whether to require certain information, such as the criteria used to determine whether a federal property was suitable for the tenant, the properties evaluated, and the factors that disqualified each property from consideration.

H.R. 2612 also includes provisions designed to monitor and control real property acquisition costs. As noted, project cost escalation has become a concern to many Members of Congress, highlighted by massive cost overruns among courthouse construction projects. The bill proposes a new requirement that may provide Congress with a "red flag" for projects at risk for significant cost escalation. This requirement—that GSA notify the authorizing committees in writing of any increase or decrease of more than 5% of the estimated maximum cost or scope or size of a project—may give Congress an opportunity to hold hearings and work with GSA to prevent further cost escalation. The 5% requirement also stipulates that GSA must provide an explanation of why a project's cost or size exceeds the amount authorized. The explanation may be useful in making revisions to the project management plan and preventing further escalation, but it also may help identify factors that contribute to escalation across projects. It was determined, for example, that courthouse costs often escalated because the method for calculating the amount of courtroom space needed was flawed, resulting in costly over-building, and GSA agreed to use a new asset management planning method for courthouses going forward.[29] Quickly identifying the factors that drive cost escalation may allow GSA to take steps to prevent similar problems in other projects.

A second cost containment measure in the bill would require GSA to notify the authorizing committees in writing before entering into certain leases that fall below the prospectus threshold. This provision would apply specifically to leases for which a prospectus is not required to be submitted and therefore have little congressional oversight. It reaffirms the principle that the government should obtain suitable space in the most cost-effective manner, regardless of the amount of funds involved. As policy, the bill would require GSA to ensure it is not paying above the local market rate for the type and amount of space being leased, even if the lease is below the prospectus threshold. With little data available on these leases, Congress may wish to request periodic audits from the GSA Inspector General or from GAO to (1) determine the extent to which GSA complies with the requirement and (2) estimate of the cost of leases that exceed local market rates.

H.R. 2612 would require additional reporting on GSA leases. Much, but not all of the information the bill would require to be reported is already made available in spreadsheets on GSA's website.[30] These lease inventory reports provide data on the size, address, tenant agency, and rental rate of GSA's leases—which represents four of the five data elements GSA would be required to report under H.R. 2612. The one required data element that GSA does not currently report is the amount authorized for leases that exceed the prospectus threshold. GSA's inventory reports also differ from the requirements of H.R. 2612 in that they are issued monthly, rather than annually, and they include data on all of GSA's active leases, not just leases entered into during the previous fiscal year. However, given that the data required by the bill are either already being reported or should be readily accessible, there should not be significant burden placed on GSA in meeting these requirements. In addition, given the limitations on oversight discussed in this report, Congress may wish to consider whether to require GSA to provide additional data, either through the report mandated by H.R. 2612 or through GSA's monthly lease inventory reports. Congress may find it useful to know, for example, the projected and actual costs invested in each lease beyond rent (i.e., upgrades and renovations), whether the lease has increased 5% in cost or size beyond authorized parameters, whether GSA has notified the authorizing committees of this increase, whether the lease has increased 10% in cost or size beyond authorized parameters, and whether an amended prospectus has been approved.

Concluding Observations

While GSA may be commonly referred to as "the government's landlord," it only controls approximately 422 million square feet in buildings, which represents about 12.6% of the government's 3.354 billion total building square footage.[31] There may be oversight provisions that would be useful if they applied to all federal landholding agencies, or at least the 24 large agencies commonly referred to as the Chief Financial Officer Act (CFO Act) agencies, which control 3.302 billion square feet in federal buildings.[32]

There are several committees that are considering real property reform bills which share some of the core objectives of H.R. 2612—reducing inventory, increasing transparency, and controlling costs—but which would apply to a broader range of federal landholders.[33] Particular provisions that do not appear in these government-wide real property reform bills but that committees might consider incorporating could include the required offset of new space, zero-based space-justification, and additional cost-escalation warnings.

By the same token, there may be provisions in active legislation which, if enacted, could provide mechanisms for implementing provisions of H.R. 2612. Several bills propose increased public reporting of agency real-property data or providing public access to GSA's Federal Real Property Profile, an existing database which contains a great deal of information about owned and leased properties government-wide. A publicly accessible, government-wide real-property database, if established, might be able to incorporate additional information as proposed in H.R. 2612, such as lease data, as well as data that are not specifically required by H.R. 2612 or other reform bills but which might be a valuable cost-assessment tool—an alternative analysis of all proposed leases which would compare the cost of leasing versus owning new space over a 20- or 30-year period.

End Notes

[1] Federal Real Property Council, FY2012 Federal Real Property Report, Appendix, p. 4.
[2] Ibid.
[3] 44 Stat. 630.
[4] 63 Stat. 176.
[5] 63 Stat. 377.
[6] 73 Stat. 479.
[7] The U.S. General Services Administration (GSA) promulgates the Federal Management Regulation (FMR), which is codified in 41 C.F.R. § 102 et seq. The FMR includes the agency's real property regulations and policies.
[8] 40 U.S.C. § 3307(a).
[9] 40 U.S.C. § 3307(h).
[10] Letter from Dan Tangherlini, General Services Administration Acting Administrator, to Senator Barbara Boxer, Chairman, Committee on Environment and Public Works, June 4, 2013.
[11] 40 U.S.C. § 3307(a).
[12] 40 U.S.C. § 3307(d).
[13] 40 U.S.C. § 3307(f).
[14] 40 U.S.C. § 3307(e).
[15] Ibid.
[16] 40 U.S.C. § 3307(c).
[17] U.S. Government Accountability Office, Federal Courthouse Construction: Better Planning, Oversight, and Courtroom Sharing Needed to Address Future Costs, GAO-10-417, June 2010, p. 9.
[18] Ibid.

[19] U.S. Government Accountability Office, High-Risk Series: An Update, GAO-13-283, February 2013, p. 107.

[20] U.S. Government Accountability Office, Federal Buildings Fund: Improved Transparency and Long-term Plan Needed to Clarify Capital Funding Priorities, GAO-12-646, July 2012, p. 4.

[21] U.S. Government Accountability Office, Federal Real Property: Greater Transparency and Strategic Focus Needed for High-Value GSA Leases, GAO-13-744, September 2013, p. 22.

[22] Ibid.

[23] U.S. General Services Administration, Office of Inspector General, Review of Management Controls over the Lease Prospectus Process, Report Number A070199/P/R/R09002, July 15, 2009, pp. 4-6.

[24] Ibid.

[25] U.S. General Services Administration, Pricing Desk Guide, April 5, 2010, p. 2-25.

[26] Federal Real Property Council, FY 2012 Federal Real Property Report, Appendix, p. 9, at http://www.gsa.gov/portal/content/102880?utm_source=OGP&utm_medium=print-radio &utm_term=frppreport&utm_campaign=shortcuts.

[27] For more information see CRS Report R43247, Disposal of Unneeded Federal Buildings: Legislative Proposals in the 113th Congress, by Garrett Hatch.

[28] U.S. General Services Administration, Realty Services, The Disposal Process, at http://www.gsa.gov/portal/content/ 101694.

[29] U.S. Government Accountability Office, Federal Courthouses: Recommended Construction Projects Should be Evaluated under New Capital-Planning Process, GAO-13-263, April 2013, pp.22-23.

[30] U.S. General Services Administration, Leasing Policy and Procedures, Lease Inventory, at http://www.gsa.gov/ portal/content/101840.

[31] Federal Real Property Council, FY 2012 Federal Real Property Report, Appendix, p. 3, at http://www.gsa.gov/portal/content/102880?utm_source=OGP&utm_medium=print-radio& utm_term=frppreport&utm_campaign=shortcuts. This figure is not comprehensive because not all federal agencies are required to report annually on their real property portfolios but it does include 24 of the largest landholders, commonly referred to as the CFO Act agencies.

[32] The 24 agencies subject to the provisions of the Chief Financial Officers Act of 1990 (P.L. 101-576, 104 Stat. 2839) are the Department of Agriculture, Department of Commerce, Department of Defense, Department of Education, Department of Energy, Department of Health and Human Services, Department of Homeland Security, Department of Housing and Urban Development, Department of the Interior, Department of Justice, Department of Labor, Department of State, Department of Transportation, Department of Treasury, Department of Veterans Affairs, Environmental Protection Agency, National Aeronautics and Space Administration, Agency for International Development, General Services Administration, National Science Foundation, Nuclear Regulatory Commission, Office of Personnel Management, Small Business Administration, and the Social Security Administration.

[33] Examples of committees considering government-wide real property reform bills include the House Committee on Oversight and Government Reform (H.R. 328, Excess Federal Building and Property Disposal Act of 2013); the House Committee on Transportation and Infrastructure (H.R. 695, Civilian Property Realignment Act of 2013); the Senate Committee on Homeland Security and Governmental Affairs (S. 1398, Federal Real Property Asset Management Reform Act of 2013 and S. 1715, Civilian Property Realignment Act of 2013, which is the companion bill to H.R. 795).

In: Federal Real Property: Analyses of Key Issues ISBN: 978-1-63482-278-7
Editor: Adam B. Clark

Chapter 2

CAPITAL FINANCING: ALTERNATIVE APPROACHES TO BUDGETING FOR FEDERAL REAL PROPERTY*

United States Government Accountability Office

ABBREVIATIONS

ARS	Agriculture Research Service
CAF	Capital Acquisition Fund
CBO	Congressional Budget Office
EUL	Enhanced Use Lease
FBF	Federal Buildings Fund
FFB	Federal Financing Bank
GSA	General Services Administration
Interior	Department of the Interior
NPS	National Park Service
OMB	Office of Management and Budget
PAYGO	Pay-as-you-go budget enforcement mechanisms
VA	Department of Veterans Affairs
VHA	Veterans Health Administration
USDA	United States Department of Agriculture

* This is an edited, reformatted and augmented version of The United States Government Accountability Office publication, GAO-14-239, dated March 2014.

WHY GAO DID THIS STUDY

Federal real property projects are fully funded when Congress provides budget authority and appropriations for the estimated full cost of the projects up front—at the time they are undertaken. However, as agencies work to balance limited resources with mission demands, many have turned to approaches other than full upfront funding to acquire, renovate, or dispose of federal real property, such as buildings, structures, and land. GAO was asked to review alternative models for managing federal real property. This report examines (1) agency experiences funding federal real property projects, (2) some of the alternative funding mechanisms selected agencies use, as well as agency experiences using selected mechanisms, and (3) alternative budgetary structures within the current unified budget that may potentially help Congress and agencies better recognize the cost of real property projects and associated returns, promoting both transparency and fiscal control. GAO reviewed case study projects from 4 agencies among the top 10 in federal real property holdings and chosen based on their use of alternative funding mechanisms, as identified in our past and ongoing work. Finally, GAO identified alternative budgetary structures that may support real property projects and principles for considering them by reviewing published reports and interviewing federal budget staff and experts.

GAO is not making any recommendations in this report. GSA, USDA, VA, and Interior generally agreed with our findings. USDA, Interior and VA provided technical comments that were incorporated as appropriate.

WHAT GAO FOUND

Officials at four selected agencies—the General Services Administration (GSA), U.S. Department of Agriculture (USDA), the Department of Veterans Affairs (VA), and the Department of the Interior (Interior)—experienced challenges receiving full upfront funding for federal real property projects through the annual appropriations process. For example, due to budget constraints, GSA acquired one property between 2008 and 2012. In addition, GSA has been unable to access funding to complete renovations in Interior's headquarters building due to obligation limitations in the GSA-administered Federal Buildings Fund (FBF). The FBF, which is the primary funding source for operating and capital costs associated with federal space, held an unobligated carryover balance of $4.7 billion at the end of fiscal year 2013 as a result of congressional limits on obligations. Officials noted that authority to retain proceeds provides a key incentive to initiate disposals, as agencies without this authority must request upfront funding for disposal costs while resulting proceeds are paid to the Department of the Treasury. Nonetheless, officials at selected agencies with the authority to retain disposal proceeds cited barriers to disposals, such as poor market demand, historical status or necessary remediation.

Instead of full upfront funding, selected agencies sometimes used a variety of alternative funding mechanisms to meet their real property needs by leveraging authorized monetary resources, such as retained fees, and non-monetary resources, such as property exchanged in a swap or space offered in an enhanced use lease. Alternative funding mechanisms are not universally available to all agencies; even within an agency, legal authorities may differ across agency components. For alternative funding mechanisms that involve working with a partner, such as in a land swap, the agency's ability to find an appropriate partner, manage that partnering relationship, and share risk—both explicit and implicit—with the partner affected project outcomes. For example, because of legal, cost, and other challenges, officials from USDA's Agricultural Research Service (ARS) said that ARS held onto land for about 10 years while seeking an appropriate partner to successfully complete the land swap.

Changes to the budgetary structure itself—within the bounds of the unified budget—might provide a more consistent way to meet real property needs while helping Congress and agencies make more prudent long-term fiscal decisions. Alternative budgetary structures should balance tradeoffs across two key GAO-identified budgeting and capital planning principles: (1) promoting transparency and fiscal control with regard to the funding of federal real property; and (2) providing agencies the flexibility to facilitate the acquisition, repair and alteration, and disposal of federal real property in support of federal missions. GAO provides alternative budgetary structure options for Congress to consider. For example, in one option Congress would make the full balance of the FBF available for funding real property projects, which could create room for additional agency flexibility but may reduce fiscal control. Another option would establish a government-wide capital acquisition fund with authority to borrow from the Federal Financing Bank for approved projects, which could improve transparency of both costs and benefits upfront and over time while business case analyses could provide a means of assuring fiscal control.

March 12, 2014

The Honorable Thomas R. Carper
Chairman
Committee on Homeland Security and Governmental Affairs
United States Senate

Dear Mr. Chairman,

The budget process is the federal government's primary resource allocation, financial planning, and control tool. Accordingly, it helps establish national spending priorities and the allocation of resources; it also helps ensure that the government spends taxpayers' money in accordance with applicable laws. Given the budget's dual functions, federal real property projects such as structures, buildings, and land are fully funded when Congress provides budget authority for the estimated full cost of projects up front (at the time they are undertaken). Such upfront funding recognizes the commitments embodied in budgetary decisions and maintains government-wide fiscal control. However, it can be challenging for agencies to make the case for such large commitments of funding as other critical needs compete for scarce federal dollars.

Congress has provided some agencies with specific authorities to use alternative funding mechanisms for the acquisition, renovation, or disposal of federal real property without full, upfront funding. Some of these alternative mechanisms allow selected agencies to meet their real property needs by leveraging other authorized resources, such as retained fees or land swaps with a private sector partner. Depending on the funding approach, the budgetary treatment of project costs may allow an agency to spread the asset cost over a number of years or monetary costs incurred may not be recognized in the budget. Because various funding approaches are reflected differently in the budget, resource allocation decisions for real property projects may not consider the full financial commitment the U.S. government is making. Further, costs for projects financed through alternative mechanisms may not be fully reflected in the budget request, whereas the costs for projects that require full upfront funding are fully reflected in the budget request. From an agency's perspective, meeting real property needs through alternative funding mechanisms can be attractive because the agency can undertake the project without first having to secure full upfront funding to cover the cost of the project. As a result, projects financed through alternative mechanisms may be selected over other equally worthy projects for which full upfront funding would be requested. From a government-wide perspective, however, the costs associated with some alternative funding mechanisms may be greater than full, upfront funding.[1]

In contrast to alternative funding mechanisms that agencies use to meet their real property needs, alternative structures within the budget, such as capital acquisition funds, have also been proposed. These proposed alternative budgetary structures serve as potential options to help agencies address their real property needs while minimizing costs to taxpayers. Ideally, any established alternative budgetary structure would reward prudent investment decisions from both an agency perspective and a long-term governmentwide perspective to maintain appropriate stewardship over federal resources.

You asked us to review alternative models for managing federal real property. This report examines (1) agency experiences funding federal real property projects; (2) some of the alternative funding mechanisms selected agencies use to help them in the acquisition, repair and alteration, and disposal of federal property, as well as agency experiences using selected alternative mechanisms; and (3) alternative budgetary structures within the current unified budget[2] that may help Congress and agencies better recognize the cost of real property projects and associated returns, and promote transparency and fiscal control in funding real property projects.

To illustrate agency experiences funding federal real property projects and the alternative financing mechanisms they used to meet their real federal property needs, we selected nongeneralizable case study projects from the following four agencies:

- General Services Administration (GSA),
- United States Department of Agriculture (USDA),
- Department of Veterans Affairs (VA), and
- Department of the Interior (Interior).

These 4 agencies are among the top 10 agencies in federal real property holdings according to the fiscal year 2012 Federal Real Property Profile and U.S. Postal Service property data.[3] We also chose to select these four agencies based on their use of alternative funding mechanisms, as identified in our past and ongoing work.[4]

From these agencies, we selected nongeneralizable case study projects that used an alternative funding mechanism from fiscal years 2008 through 2012.

Projects were selected based on agency data on real property projects, the dollar value of transactions, and analysis of interviews with agency officials. In some cases, projects were selected from subcomponents to illustrate use of available legal authorities. These projects are for illustrative purposes only and reflect variation in alternative funding mechanisms, but the results from these projects cannot be generalized more broadly. Selected case study projects are drawn from leases and acquisitions held and managed by GSA and the following agency subcomponents:

- Interior, National Park Service (NPS),
- USDA, Agricultural Research Service (ARS),
- USDA, Forest Service, and
- VA, Veterans Health Administration (VHA).

To understand selected agencies' experiences obtaining funding for real property projects and using alternative funding mechanisms, we analyzed relevant documentation related to agencies' real property projects. This included agency policies, budget documents, and reports to Congress. We reviewed relevant federal laws, regulations, and policies and analyzed relevant legal authorities. We interviewed cognizant officials at each of the selected agencies about their experiences obtaining funding for real property projects and using alternative funding mechanisms. We also interviewed officials involved in the selected real property projects. These nongeneralizable case studies were chosen to illustrate a range of alternative funding mechanisms. To develop themes and examples from our documentary and testimonial evidence, we analyzed information from relevant documents and interviews to identify and confirm common patterns across our selected agencies. We did not independently verify the descriptions or outcomes of the real property projects nor did we interview organizations that partnered with agencies.

Finally, to guide our consideration of alternative budgetary structures, we reviewed published reports and interviewed federal budget staff and experts. To identify principles that could help Congress and agencies recognize the cost of real property projects and associated returns, and promote transparency and fiscal control in funding real property projects, we reviewed our prior reports and external sources, such as Office of Management and Budget (OMB) guidance and the report of the President's Commission on Budget Concepts. We then reviewed our reports and external literature to identify funding structures that could help support real property projects. From this review, we identified and explored various options which we compared to proposed changes within the current unified budget. We also used this literature to identify possible implications—a list which is not exhaustive—if identified options were to be adopted. We then interviewed federal budget staff from the Congressional Budget Office (CBO) and OMB as well as industry experts to obtain their views on the benefits and challenges of the alternative budgetary structures that we identified. We contacted the National Federal Development Association, a trade association representing organizations and individuals that provide real estate services to the federal government. This association referred us to an industry expert with more than 25 years of experience in federal government real estate.

In addition, we spoke with a past congressional witness with extensive experience on federal real estate and budgeting experience at both OMB and CBO. Finally, we shared these alternative budgetary structures with our selected agencies to obtain their views.

We conducted this performance audit from May 2013 to March 2014 in accordance with generally accepted government auditing standards. Those standards require that we plan and perform the audit to obtain sufficient, appropriate evidence to provide a reasonable basis for our findings and conclusions based on our audit objectives. We believe that the evidence obtained provides a reasonable basis for our findings and conclusions based on our audit objectives.

BACKGROUND

Since 2003, we have identified managing federal real property, including effectively managing excess and underused property and an overreliance on leasing, as a high risk issue facing the federal government. In June 2010, the President directed agencies to achieve real property cost savings through a number of measures, including disposal of excess real property and reducing leasing through consolidations and increased space utilization.[5] In 2011, the administration proposed legislation, known as the Civilian Property Realignment Act (commonly referred to as CPRA), and accompanying bills were introduced in both legislative chambers, which would identify opportunities to consolidate, reduce, and realign the federal footprint as well as expedite the disposal of properties by building off the military base realignment and closure (commonly referred to as BRAC) processes.[6] In May 2012, OMB issued a memorandum directing agencies to not increase the size of their civilian real estate inventory, stating that increases in an agency's total square footage of civilization property must be offset through consolidation, co-location, or disposal of space from the inventory of that agency, a policy that became known as "freeze the footprint." As a result, acquisition has become more about consolidation and identifying opportunities to share space rather than acquiring new space.

Pursuant to the Government Performance and Results Modernization Act, OMB identified real property as a Federal Government priority goal.[7] Agencies are currently working on 3-year Revised Real Property Cost Savings and Innovation Plans to maintain the fiscal year 2012 square footage baseline for federal office and warehouse inventory. Agencies have been encouraged to work collaboratively with other agencies and GSA to find opportunities for smarter space usage through co-locations and consolidations. We have previously reported that real property decisions draw considerable attention during congressional deliberations over federal appropriations. Stakeholders such as Congress, OMB, and the real property-holding agencies have an interest in how the federal government carries out its real property acquisition, management, and disposal practices.[8]

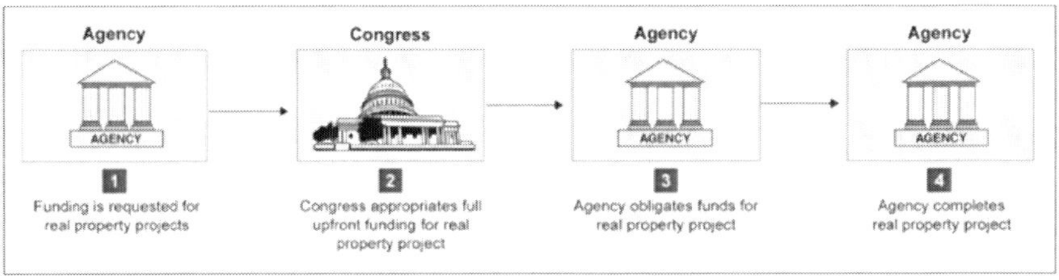

Source: GAO analysis.

Figure 1. The Process of Obtaining Upfront Funding through the Annual Appropriations Process.

Ideally, when an agency has a real property need, such as repairing or altering its headquarters building, it determines how to meet that need through internal prioritization and the capital planning process. As part of the capital funding process, shown in Figure 1, an agency prepares a business case analysis and considers how to fund the project, including whether to request upfront funding. If an agency chooses to request upfront funding from Congress, it submits a business case to Congress through the annual appropriations process. If Congress approves the project, it may authorize spending for the project by appropriating full upfront funding to the agency.

Once an agency has obtained upfront funding, it can obligate funds to complete "useful assets"[9] of the project. During implementation as well as at completion of the project, an agency may realize returns, such as proceeds from disposal. The completion of the project informs agency prioritization and ongoing planning for future real property projects.

Budget Scorekeeping

Budget scorekeeping rules are meant to recognize costs as funding decisions are being made. These rules were established to ensure that the scorekeepers—that is, the House and Senate Budget Committees, the CBO, and OMB—can measure the effects of legislation consistently and conclude that they meet specific legal requirements. These rules are also used by OMB for determining amounts to be recognized in the budget when an agency signs a contract or enters into a lease.

Scorekeeping in the Federal Budget

What is scorekeeping?

Scorekeeping is the process of estimating the budgetary effects of pending legislation and comparing them to a baseline. The process allows Congress to compare the cost of proposed budgetary policy changes to existing law and to enforce spending and revenue levels agreed upon in the budget resolution.

Who are the scorekeepers?

Guidelines are established by the OMB, the CBO, and the Senate and House Budget Committees. Scorekeepers have an ongoing dialogue and may revise rules as required. Budget Committees and CBO apply the rules to estimate the costs associated with proposed legislation. OMB uses the rules to determine amounts to be recognized in the budget when an agency signs a contract or enters into a lease. The House and Senate Budget Committees make available monthly summary scorekeeping reports.

Source: GAO analysis of Title 2 of the U.S. Code and OMB guidance.

We have previously found that upfront funding is the best way to ensure recognition of commitments embodied in budgeting decisions and maintain government-wide fiscal control.[10] As shown below, under scorekeeping rules, for a purchase or a capital lease the full cost of the project must be recorded in the budget in the year in which the budget authority is to be made available.[11] In contrast, operating leases are intended for short-term needs, and under the scorekeeping rules, only the amount needed to cover the first year's lease payments plus cancellation costs need to be recorded in the budget in that year.

Summary of Scorekeeping Guidelines for Purchases and Leases

When an agency is granted the authority to enter into a contract for the purchase, lease-purchase, capital lease, or operating lease of an asset, budget authority and outlays may be scored as follows:

- *Lease-purchases and Capital Leases:* budget authority will be scored against the legislation in the year in which the budget authority is first made available in the amount of the estimated net present value of the government's total estimated legal obligations over the life of the contract, except for imputed interest and identifiable operating expenses.
- *Operating leases:* budget authority will be scored against the legislation in the year in which the budget authority is first made available in the amount necessary to cover the government's legal obligation. The amount scored will include the estimated total payments expected to arise under the full term of the lease contract, or, if a cancellation clause is included in the lease, for the first fiscal year and the amount of cancellation costs.[12]
- *Purchases:* no special rules apply to scoring purchases of assets (whether the asset is existing or is to be manufactured or constructed). Budget authority is scored in the year in which the authority to purchase is first made available in the amount of the government's estimated legal obligations.

To distinguish lease purchases and capital leases from operating leases, the following criteria will be used for defining an operating lease:

- Ownership of the asset remains with the lessor during the term of the lease and is not transferred to the government at or shortly after the end of the lease period.

- The lease does not contain a bargain-price purchase option.
- The lease term does not exceed 75 percent of the estimated economic lifetime of the asset.
- The present value of the minimum lease payments over the life of the lease does not exceed 90 percent of the fair market value of the asset at the inception of the lease.
- The asset is a general purpose asset rather than being for a special purpose of the government and is not built to unique specification for the government as lessee.
- There is a private-sector market for the asset.

Source: GAO analysis of OMB Circular No. A-11

Using an operating lease—or successive operating leases—for a longterm space need may result in resource allocation decisions for which the budgeting process may not have considered the full financial commitment over the full length of time the space need exists. Consequently, costly operating leases may appear on paper to be preferable to less-costly alternatives such as major construction or renovation projects that must compete for full funding.

GSA's Role

Within the vast portfolio of government owned and leased assets, GSA plays the role of broker and property manager to many federal civilian agencies, although some agencies—including USDA, VA, and Interior— have independent authority related to real property. GSA has a large portfolio of federally-owned and leased properties that it rents to its federal agency customers. As of fiscal year 2011, GSA had a total of 374.6 million rentable square feet in its inventory, of which 192.7 million— slightly more than half— were leased.

The Federal Buildings Fund (FBF), administered by GSA, is a fund established by the Public Buildings Act Amendments of 1972. The FBF is the primary source of funds for operating and capital costs associated with federal space. The FBF is funded primarily by income from rental charges assessed to tenant agencies occupying federally owned and GSA-managed and -leased space that approximate commercial rates for comparable space and services.[13] Congress exercises control over the FBF through the appropriations process that sets annual limits on how much of the fund can be obligated for various activities. In addition, it periodically provides supplemental appropriations for the Fund. For example, the Fund received $5.6 billion as part of the American Recovery and Reinvestment Act of 2009.[14] GSA may incur obligations and make expenditures from the FBF in five categories of activities: (1) rental of space, (2) repairs and alterations, (3) construction and acquisition of facilities, (4) building operations and maintenance, and (5) installment acquisition payments (funds debt incurred as the result of building acquisition and lease purchase arrangements). Revenue from the federally-owned facility inventory managed by GSA is the main source of the FBF's operating income used to fund repair and alteration, new construction activities, and operations and maintenance. By statute, GSA is required to provide a prospectus for each proposed lease with a net annual rent above the prospectus threshold—$2.79 million in fiscal year 2013, which GSA's Administrator is authorized to adjust annually—or capital project over that threshold, including acquisition, new construction, and repair and alteration projects. As shown in Figure 2, each prospectus is reviewed and approved by both OMB and Congressional authorizing committees.

GSA has not conducted 30-year present value analyses as part of its prospectus process since the mid-1990s, as advised by OMB. Such analyses help weigh the cost over time of leasing versus owning an asset to promote efficient resource allocation for the civilian agencies within GSA's real property portfolio. In September 2013 we reported that the decision to halt this type of formal analysis for high-value leases has limited the transparency of the prospectus process. We recommended that lease prospectuses include a description of the length of time an agency estimates a need for a space, how long the agency has leased that particular space, and major investments necessary. For spaces for which an agency has a long-term projected need, we recommended that GSA include an appropriate form of cost-to-lease versus cost-to-own analysis. GSA concurred with this recommendation.[15] Although at times leasing versus owning analyses found leasing to be a more cost effective option, it often concluded that ownership would be cheaper than leasing; however, in many cases where ownership was found to be the better option, GSA ultimately recommended leasing due to funding constraints.[16]

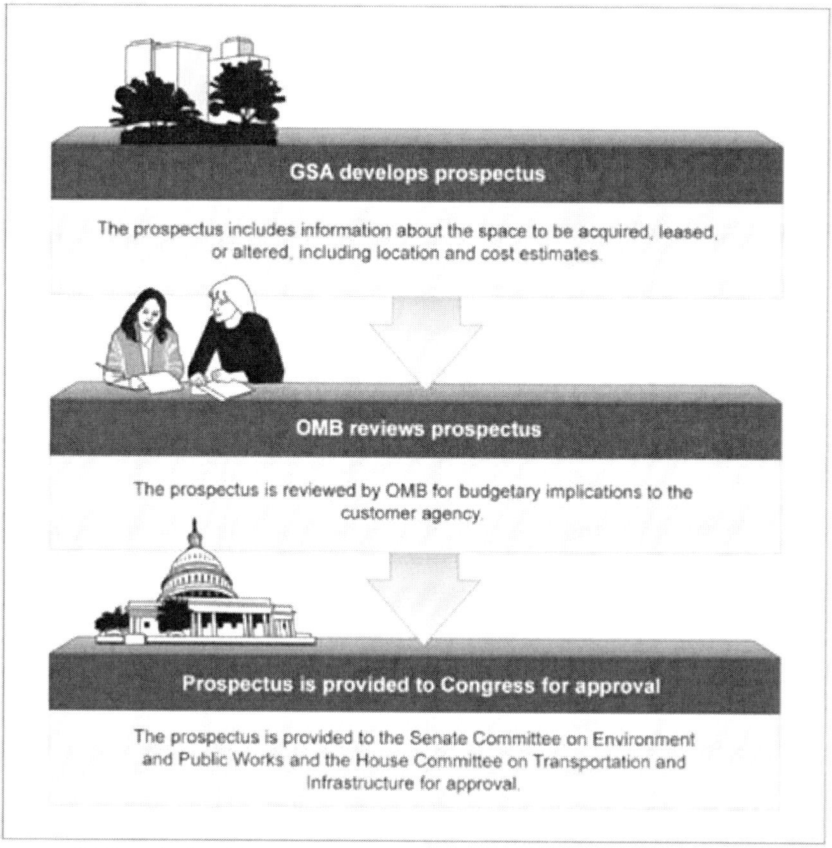

Source: GAO analysis of GSA data.

Figure 2. Prospectus Process for Approval of High-Value Federal Building Fund Transactions.

Case Study Agency Officials Experienced Challenges Receiving Full Upfront Funding for Federal Real Property Projects

Officials at four selected agencies—GSA, USDA, VA, and Interior—experienced challenges receiving full upfront funding for federal real property projects through the annual appropriations process. For example, GSA officials told us that obtaining upfront funding through appropriations is difficult and thus presents a barrier to ownership, resulting in a reliance on leased space.[17] USDA officials said that, given current fiscal pressures, they do not routinely request acquisition funds. Interior officials told us that the Department has had a moratorium on new construction since 2010 and that any upfront funding received through the annual appropriations process goes towards necessary renovations to existing property. Although VA requests and receives appropriations for some real property construction projects, it has a significant backlog of incomplete major construction projects that have not received funding. The Veteran's Health Administration (VHA) requested $215 million for major construction funding in fiscal year 2014 and estimates that it would require $5.8 billion to address its current backlog.

Budget constraints have resulted in limited acquisitions at GSA, Interior, and USDA. For example, GSA's sole acquisition between 2008 and 2012 resulted from exercising a purchase option on a preexisting lease. GSA renewed its lease at Columbia Plaza in Washington, D.C. for the Department of State (State) in 1992.[18] As part of an agreement to invest $30.6 million in renovations to the building at that time, GSA was directed by congressional resolution to "attempt to include a purchase option in the lease contract." GSA did not have the option to purchase the building in 1992 but it negotiated a purchase option as part of the terms of the 20- year lease. As the expiration of the lease neared, GSA concluded that a mission need for the building remained and that acquiring the building would be financially advantageous. Under the original contract, GSA could purchase the building for $100 million though the 2009 appraised value was $150 million. A 30-year present value analysis concluded that acquiring the building would result in an annual cost advantage of $12 million over continuing to lease and, in 2012, GSA exercised its purchase option. Because State was already occupying Columbia Plaza, GSA officials said that they mitigated a portion of the acquisition cost by avoiding certain costs typical to the construction process including acquiring land, phased funding for construction, paying for interim office space, and final relocation to the new space. However, purchase options may cost more over the life of a lease than buying a building upfront.[19] Figure 3 shows that although the contract purchase price was $100 million, adding in the initial renovation costs and lease payments made over the 20-year term, in total the acquisition cost to the government was $258 million.

Limitations on obligations constrain funding for real property, especially for repairs, alterations, and new construction. The difference between receipts collected in the FBF and the amount authorized for annual obligations affected one of our case study agencies that rents property through GSA.

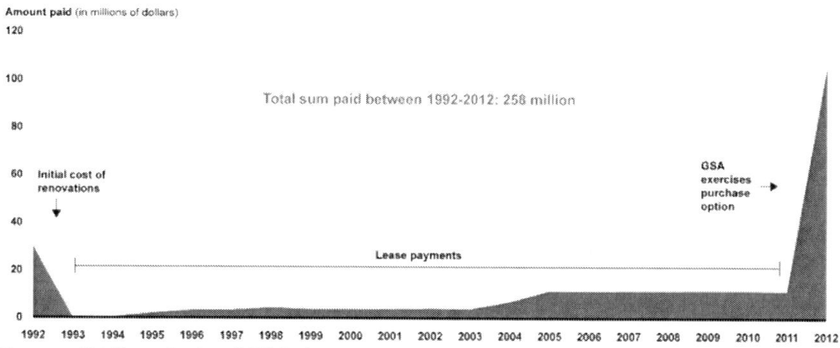

Source: GAO analysis of GSA data.

[a] Rental data excludes tax reimbursements.

[b] Fiscal year 2012 includes both lease payments made in that year and the property purchase price.

Figure 3. Total Costs for Columbia Plaza Transaction Included Initial Renovations and Lease Payments.

Interior officials said that GSA has been unable to obtain FBF funding through the annual appropriations process to complete renovations in Interior's federally-owned and GSA-managed headquarters building. As a result, Interior officials said that they have not been able to realize the savings they anticipated for a full renovation, such as energy savings. The FBF's balance has increased significantly in recent years, growing from $56 million at the beginning of fiscal year 2007 to $4.7 billion at the end of fiscal year 2013.[20] As we previously reported, the increased balance has primarily resulted from the growing difference between the resources deposited into the FBF and the level of funds GSA is authorized to spend. GSA officials noted that when Congress provides less obligational authority than requested, repairs, alterations, and new construction projects for GSA-managed buildings are most affected because available funds are first used to pay leasing, operations and maintenance, and debt costs. As a result, GSA's obligations authority for repairs and alterations projects decreased from $855 million in 2005 to $280 million in 2012.[21] GSA officials noted that when prioritizing requests for repair and alteration projects, they consider asset condition and performance; life safety and compliance with laws and regulations; customer considerations, including consolidation and reduction in space; financial viability, including lease cost avoidance; and improvements to utilization rates and recapturing vacant space.

With regard to the disposal of federal property, officials at USDA, which has authority to retain proceeds from sales and disposals, cited financial obstacles to these initiatives, such as little market demand. For example, USDA's Forest Service was given authority in 2005 to retain proceeds from disposals;[22] it typically uses these funds for critical maintenance work on its properties or to prepare other buildings for sale. Forest Service officials said that except for a few administrative buildings in affluent areas sold for a high return, the return on investment for disposals, often for structures on land Forest Service would like to retain, is minimal. In 2011, the Forest Service reported that it would cost $120 million to dispose of property with a salvage value of $5 million.

Non-financial barriers to disposal also exist, resulting in underused agency property. These obstacles include remote locations, necessary environmental cleanup, or limitations on the use of property. Historically significant properties are also challenges. For example, VA officials said that VA's historical buildings often require significant cleanup and preparation prior to disposal, and the agency must often address significant stakeholder interests. In addition, VHA's buildings are often on campuses or are medical facilities, limiting potential buyers or lessees to those with missions similar to VA. VHA currently has about 250 vacant buildings with no defined need, totaling more than 4 million square feet.

Interior officials stated that the land Interior owns is primarily stewardship land for preservation, and thus Interior has few buildings or land to sell. Instead, excess buildings on stewardship lands are typically demolished. To facilitate the disposal of excess property, Interior includes funding for disposals as part of its planning process—it requires each bureau to set aside 3 percent of its property budget for disposals of excess property.

Officials at GSA and USDA noted that the authority to retain proceeds provides a key incentive to initiate disposal transactions. For example, officials at GSA, which provides disposal services across the federal government, stated that the vast majority of current disposal transactions are by agencies or components that have the authority to retain the proceeds from sales or disposals. They also said that agencies without this authority may have less incentive to dispose of underused property as they must take money from competing budget priorities to invest in readying a property for sale. USDA officials said that because resulting proceeds are remitted to the general fund of the U.S. Treasury as miscellaneous receipts, components without authority to retain proceeds have little incentive to request full upfront funding for disposal costs such as site cleanup, resource surveys, title and legal preparation, and auction fees.

ALTERNATIVE FUNDING MECHANISMS HELPED AGENCIES MEET THEIR REAL PROPERTY NEEDS, BUT ALSO POSED CHALLENGES

Agencies Use a Variety of Funding Mechanisms to Meet Their Real Property Needs

Selected agencies have been authorized to use a variety of funding mechanisms as an alternative to full upfront funding to meet their real property needs. Funding mechanisms leverage both monetary resources, such as retained fees, and non-monetary resources, such as property exchanged in a land swap or space offered in an enhanced use lease (EUL).[23] In some cases, the funding mechanism may function as a public-private partnership intended to further an agency's mission by working with a partner to leverage resources. Some of these mechanisms allow the private sector to provide the project's capital—at their cost of borrowing. The U.S. federal government's cost of borrowing is lower than in the private sector. When the private sector provides the project capital, the federal government later repays these higher private sector borrowing costs (e.g., in the form of lease payments). In some cases, factors such as lower labor costs or fewer requirements could potentially help balance the higher cost of borrowing, making partner financing less expensive. Table 1 outlines selected funding mechanisms, considerations for each mechanism based on our past work, and examples of mechanisms used by the selected agencies.

Table 1. Selected Alternative Funding Mechanism Definitions, Considerations, and Related Case Studies

Mechanisms	Considerations based on past work	Case study examples	Case study outcomes
Operating lease used to meet long-term need			

Table 1. (Continued)

Mechanisms	Considerations based on past work	Case study examples	Case study outcomes
Operating lease used to meet long-term need			
An operating lease gives the federal government the use of an asset for a specified period of time, but the ownership of the asset does not change. While there are no specific time limits, an operating lease is not intended to be used for long-term property needs.	When used as intended for short-term needs, operating leases are not alternative funding mechanisms. However, operating leases—or successive operating leases—have been used to help acquire assets for which there is a long-term need, resulting in inefficient resource allocation decisions.[a] Operating leases used to consolidate space may require upfront costs (i.e., moving, space reconfiguration, furniture) but may result in long-term cost savings from decreased rental costs.[b]	GSA: Operating Lease for NPS in Washington, DC NPS relocated to leased space due to the renovation of Interior's Headquarters in the early 2000s. In 2002, GSA consolidated multiple NPS components to 1201 Eye Street, NW, Washington D.C. GSA was approved through the prospectus process to extend the lease in 2012 for 15 more years and utilize the space more efficiently.	GSA acquired leased space needed to help transition NPS to federally owned space. GSA is exploring opportunities to reduce costs by moving the entire NPS requirement into federally owned space.
		GSA: Operating lease for NPS in Lakewood, Colorado Although GSA considered construction, GSA entered into a replacement operating lease in Lakewood, Colorado, which allowed NPS to consolidate offices in	NPS annual lease payments were over $1.3 million less than requestedin the prospectus.

Mechanisms	Considerations based on past work	Case study examples	Case study outcomes
		2 locations into one office with more efficient space utilization.	
Land swap			
A real property swap is an exchange of property owned by the federal government with either a private entity or a state or local government for another property.	Use of land swaps is limited by the need for well-aligned mutual needs. Land swaps are generally non-cash transactions and thus are not recognized in the budget.[c] Property swaps can relieve the federal government of maintenance and/or renovation costs and result in a real asset that may be used immediately with no additional appropriations required. However, determining fair value for the properties exchanged is not always a clear-cut process and congressional oversight of these exchanges is limited.[d]	USDA, ARS: Land swap with city of Ames, Iowa ARS exchanged land with the city of Ames, Iowa to meet its need for land near its facility outside the city of Ames to use for the disposal of manure from diseased animals used in experiments. ARS had land in Ames it could not use for this purpose that the city of Ames sought to use to build a new water treatment plant. The city acquired land for the sole purpose of completing the exchange with ARS.	ARS was able to dispose of excess property in one location and acquire land better situated for its needs. ARS officials reported that the land swap was more efficient and environmentally sustainable than building an expensive incinerator. A land swap requires both a land disposal process and an acquisition process. As a result, ARS officials noted it was time intensive.

Table 1. (Continued)

Mechanisms	Considerations based on past work	Case study examples	Case study outcomes
		VA, VHA: Land swap with city of New Orleans, Louisiana The New Orleans Replacement VA Medical Center Project will construct a new medical center to replace one damaged in Hurricane Katrina. The city of New Orleans, through Louisiana State University on behalf of the state of Louisiana, acquired voluntarily and when necessary through eminent domain approximately 30 acres of downtown New Orleans property that it transferred to VA. In return, VA will transfer the existing damaged medical center to the city following activation of the new medical center.	The land swap allowed VAto continue providing medical services while the new facility was under construction. The city of New Orleans worked with the state of Louisiana to obtain the property that the city swapped with VA voluntarily and when necessary through eminent domain, ensuring the availability of appropriate space.
Retained fees			
Proceeds that result from business-type or market-oriented activities with the public, such as the collection of	The legislation authorizing these fees may assign them for a specific purpose without further Congressional action or require them to be	Interior, NPS: Herring Cove Beach and Nauset Light Beach in Provincetown and Eastham, Massachusetts	Officials reported that using retained fees allowed NPS to completehigh priority repairs more quickly than if NPS had requested appropriated funds.

Mechanisms	Considerations based on past work	Case study examples	Case study outcomes
user fees.	appropriated in annual appropriation acts before they can be spent. In some cases, agencies have been authorized to retain earned fees to fund capital projects and improvements.[e]	NPS used recreation fees to fund repairs designed to protect the facilities from beach erosion, improve pavement and outdoor amenities, and replace the septic system. The building was renovated with new energy efficient features and moved further back from the shoreline.	
Enhanced use lease (EUL)			
An EUL allows an agency to lease out property and receive payment in cash or in kind (goods or services that result in direct cost savings to the government) from the lessee.	The agency acts as the lessor– rather than lessee. The project is limited by the need to find an appropriate partner.[f]	VA, VHA: Transitional Housing and Homeless Support Services in Dayton, Ohio The VA leased excess space to the Volunteers of America of Greater Ohio. The lessee renovated, operated, and maintained one building on property leased from VA. In addition to lease payments, the lessee provided 50 units of transitional housing beds and related supportive services to eligible veterans and non-veterans.	VA was able to avoid costs associated with building maintenance, property maintenance,and outpatient and domiciliary services.

Source: GAO analysis of documentation and interviews from selected agencies, the Office of Management and Budget, and prior GAO work.

[a] For example, see GAO-13-744.

[b] For example, see GAO-13-744.

[c] For example, see GAO-03-1011.

[d] For example, see GAO-03-1011.
[e] For example, see GAO-03-1011.
[f] See for example GAO, Federal Real Property: Progress Made in Reducing Unneeded Property, but VA Needs Better Information to Make Further Reductions, GAO-08-939 (Washington, D.C.: Sep. 10, 2008) and GAO, Congressionally Chartered Organizations: Key Principles for Leveraging Nonfederal Resources, GAO-13-549 (Washington, D.C.: June. 7, 2013).

Alternative funding mechanisms are not universally available to all agencies. Moreover, even within an agency, legal authorities may differ across agency components. For example, the Forest Service and ARS— both components of USDA—have different legal authorities to use alternative funding mechanisms. For example, the Forest Service has the authority to retain fees and ARS has the authority to enter into land swaps.

Instead of upfront funding, NPS uses retained recreation fees to fund high-priority projects linked to visitor need. NPS's recreation fees, which are authorized by the Federal Land Recreation Enhancement Act, require that not less than 80 percent of retained recreation fees be spent at the site at which fees are collected while the remaining 20 percent is pooled to fund projects that are national priorities. This 20 percent of the retained recreation fees provides NPS additional flexibility. In 2011 Interior determined that it would request line item construction funds in fiscal year 2014, but later identified fiscal year 2012 funds from an alternative funding mechanism, retained recreation fees, for the Herring Cove and Nauset Light Beach facilities renovations in Massachusetts, negating the need to seek additional funding. Interior has internal processes for prioritizing projects for line item budget requests and for allocating the retained recreation fees to high-priority projects, which NPS officials reported allowed Interior to complete the renovations more quickly than would have otherwise been possible with full upfront funding.

In 1991, Congress authorized VA to enter into EULs. VA's available legal authorities also framed its 2008 decision to enter into an EUL with a nonprofit organization in Dayton, Ohio. VHA's partner in the EUL leveraged nonfederal funds to renovate a building and provide housing and services to homeless veterans. The Dayton, Ohio Veterans Affairs Medical Center had underused historic buildings. Officials reported that the buildings' historic status made it difficult to dispose of or demolish the buildings.[24] The Volunteers of America of Greater Ohio approached VA about entering into an EUL; they agreed to provide 50 beds of transitional housing and related services to homeless veterans in the property that VA wanted to take off its inventory in exchange for financial and nonfinancial considerations. VA determined that renovating the building with appropriated funds would result in the highest upfront costs to VA and would forgo the benefit of any private-sector funding or participation. VA accepted the Volunteers of America's proposal and the Volunteers of America paid VA rent for the space and were responsible for renovating, operating, and maintaining the building as well as for providing housing and services to homeless veterans. By partnering with the Volunteers of America on this EUL, VA estimated that it has cumulatively achieved almost $2.8 million in cost avoidance and that the project has provided services valued at more than $2 million while costing the VA less than $500,000. Without the authority to enter into EULs or other alternative funding mechanisms, VA officials said that VA would not have been able to move forward with this project. VA's EUL authority was amended in 2012. VA may no longer accept in-kind consideration for EULs and may only enter into an EUL for the provision of supportive housing.[25]

Risk Sharing, Managing Stakeholder Relationships, and Other Factors Affect Project Outcomes

Projects with alternative funding mechanisms involve multiple forms of risk—both implicit and explicit—that must be shared between the agency and any partner or stakeholder. We have previously reported that project decisions should reflect both the likely risk and the organization's tolerance for risk. Incorporating risk assessment and risk management practices into decisions can help ensure that the organization recognizes and is prepared to manage explicit risks (e.g., financial and physical) and implicit risks (e.g., reputational).[26] For example, clearly defined lease terms helped VA manage financial risk associated with the Dayton, Ohio EUL when its partner sought to share costs for unexpected building repairs for the building leased. During renovation, asbestos was discovered in the building and VA's partner sought a financial contribution from VA to help offset some of the cost of the cleanup. Because the contract clearly held the partner financially responsible for unexpected expenses, VA was not liable for the cleanup costs.

We have also previously reported that when working with a partner, it is important to actively manage the relationship.[27] Formalizing collaborations between the partners, including documenting dispute resolution processes, can enable productive partner interactions. For example, VA stepped in to more actively engage its partner, the city of New Orleans, in a land swap to build a hospital after Hurricane Katrina. To monitor project timelines and goals, officials representing all partners—including VA's Chief of Staff, the logistics manager and city counterparts—participated in a steering group. When it became apparent that the city of New Orleans was unable to meet its initial goal of having the property in construction-ready condition within 1 year as outlined in a memorandum of understanding (MOU), the group began to meet weekly. VA and the city of New Orleans amended the MOU to permit phased delivery of the construction ready site. Additionally, New Orleans VA Medical Center continued to have quarterly meetings with the community. Officials reported that early coordination contributed to increased efficiency and improved outcomes and helped the project overcome challenges such as managing to meet different federal and state fiscal years and funding cycles, as well as different federal, state, and local policies.

In addition to an agency's ability to share risk and manage stakeholder relationships, the availability of an appropriate partner and the geographic location of the property may affect the use and success of an alternative funding mechanism. We have previously reported that partners should bring complementary resources, skills, and financial capacities to the relationship.[28] Agency officials reported that the geographic location and the condition of a property can make it difficult to locate a willing buyer and expensive to dispose of the property. For example, according to Forest Service officials, many of the structures that may be disposed of are of little value and are on land Forest Service will retain, such as a cabin in the woods. Additionally, these facilities may be located in remote areas that are difficult and costly to access with the construction equipment necessary for demolition. As part of the auction process, Forest Service typically asks for bids at salvage value and requires that the structure be removed from the property at the buyer's expense. However, because of the expense to the buyer of the building removal and any necessary environmental remediation, properties are usually sold for low prices. The Forest Service benefits from selling the property— even for a low value— because it is no longer financially responsible for costs such as maintenance, demolition, property removal, and environmental remediation. For example, ARS needed to acquire land or build an incinerator to dispose of excess manure. ARS does not have the legal authority to purchase land valued at more than $100 and the incinerator would have been significantly more expensive than this limit, prompting ARS to consider a land swap. Because of these legal, cost, and anticipated stakeholder challenges, ARS officials said that ARS held onto the land for about 10 years while seeking an appropriate partner with whom to exchange land. When ARS identified an appropriate partner, it completed a land swap with the city of Ames, Iowa. ARS officials reported that this outcome was more efficient and environmentally friendly than the alternative of building an expensive incinerator.

ALTERNATIVE BUDGETARY STRUCTURES HAVE POTENTIAL TO HELP CONGRESS AND AGENCIES RECOGNIZE THE COSTS AND RETURNS OF REAL PROPERTY PROJECTS UPFRONT AND OVER TIME

While different funding mechanisms have been used as an alternative to obtaining upfront funding for federal real property projects, changes to the budgetary structure itself—within the bounds of the unified budget that encompasses the full scope of federal programs and transactions—may also help agencies meet their real property needs.[29] Alternative budgetary structures may be established to change budgetary incentives for agencies and therefore help Congress and agencies make more prudent long-term fiscal decisions. Such alternatives may include changing existing or introducing new account structures to fund real property projects.[30] These alternatives could promote more complete consideration of the full costs of projects and associated returns over time as well as provide agencies with greater flexibility to manage their real property needs. This could be aided by agencies completing comprehensive business case analyses detailing project costs and returns in a process similar to GSA's prospectus process.[31] A business case analysis might include details about how the project aligns with an agency's strategic plan, a needs assessment and gap identification, an alternatives evaluation, a life-cycle cost analysis, a schedule of project milestones and deliverables, and a cost-benefit analysis.[32]

> Within the *discretionary budget structure*, Congress provides budget authority for programs in annual appropriations acts. On the *mandatory side of the budget*, Congress provides budget authority for programs in laws other than annual appropriations acts.
>
> Source: GAO-05-734SP

We explored options for changes within the current discretionary budget structure and options on the mandatory side of the budget by reviewing our past reports and discussing possible options with federal budget specialists and industry experts. We make no recommendations with respect to adopting these options. However, understanding the tradeoffs associated with different aspects of alternative budgetary structures can provide decision makers with more information and support decisions about funding federal real property projects.

Budgeting and Capital Planning Principles Offer a Framework for Considering Alternative Budgetary Structures

To assist congressional and agency-level decision makers in considering alternative budgetary structures, we identified two key budgeting and capital planning principles. An alternative budgetary structure should do two things: promote transparency and fiscal control with regard to the funding of federal real property projects; and provide agencies the flexibility to facilitate the acquisition, repair and alteration, and disposal of federal real property in support of federal missions.

The two principles are each further supported by elements that may help frame the consideration of alternative budgetary structures. As decision makers consider these budgetary structures, they must balance tradeoffs between the two principles to understand whether the options would allow for full upfront cost recognition, establish accountability mechanisms to track cost recovery and return on investment, and provide timely funding to promote an appropriately sized federal real property inventory. The principles may interact and conflict with each other and each alternative budgetary structure has benefits and challenges. Moreover, the weight that different decision makers might place on the principles will vary, depending on the desired level of involvement. Table 2 provides an overview of the principles.

Table 2. Principles for Considering Changes to the Current Budgetary Structure

Principle	Elements	Why this is important
Promote transparency and fiscal control with regard to the funding of federal real property projects	Allow for recognizing full costs when "useful assets"[a] are acquired and the associated	Understanding whether costs and benefits are recognized upfront would allow Congress and agencies to compare the costs and benefits of proposed

Principle	Elements	Why this is important
	returns for the real property project	projects,would result in the recognition of actual costs to taxpayers, and would inform the level of oversight required by Congress.
	Establish accountability mechanisms to track the realization of estimated returns (e.g., cost savings and cost avoidance)	Understanding whether anticipated returns (e.g., cost savings and cost avoidance) would be realized would allow policymakers and agencies to have some assurance of cost recovery and return on investment.
Provide flexibility to facilitate the acquisition, repair/alteration, and disposal of federal real property in support of federal missions	Provide timely resources to support mission needs	Understanding whether the alternative budgetary structure would facilitate funding for real property projects in a timely manner may enable agencies to better plan and manage project funding and avoid certain costly project delays.
	Promote appropriate size of federal real property inventory, including collaborating when possible	Understanding whether the alternative budgetary structure would enable agencies to work collaboratively to co-locate and consolidate space would inform assessment of how agencies can more efficiently use space and facilitate funding for such purposes as well as facilitate opportunities to partner with other stakeholders.

Source: GAO, the President's Commission on Budget Concepts, and OMB guidance on budgeting and capital planning.

[a] A useful asset is an economically and programmatically separate segment of procuring an asset or whole asset. The total asset procurement may include one or more useful assets. Preparation, Submission, and Execution of the Budget, app. J OMB Circular No. A-11 (2013).

Discretionary Budget Authority Options Could Provide a Straightforward Means of Dedicating Funding to Real Property Projects

Changes to the current discretionary structure for funding federal real property projects may provide a relatively straightforward means of dedicating funding to federal real property while creating room for additional agency flexibility. However, tradeoffs are inherent in budgeting and these changes may affect spending for other discretionary programs competing for mission critical resources.

Modify the FBF: The FBF is a discretionary fund that receives revenue through rental payments from agencies that lease buildings that GSA manages. GSA's authority to access these funds is determined through the annual appropriations process. As previously described, resources deposited into the FBF have exceeded the amount that Congress has appropriated to GSA in recent years, resulting in a $4.7 billion difference between the full balance of the FBF and amounts made available for spending in fiscal year 2013. Congress provides authority to GSA to incur obligations and make expenditures from the FBF in five categories of activities, such as repairing and altering GSA-managed buildings and constructing new buildings. However, GSA officials said that because available funds must first be used to pay costs associated with other authorized activities, such as leasing privately owned space, operations and maintenance of GSA-managed buildings, and debt incurred from building acquisitions and lease purchase arrangements, repairs and alterations and new construction are the most affected. For example, GSA's obligational authority for repairs and alterations projects decreased from $855 million in 2005 to $280 million in 2012.[33] As a result, customer agencies are being charged for services that the GSA may be limited in its ability to provide in a timely manner. To meet agencies' real property needs, the FBF could be modified in the following ways:

- *Make the full balance of the FBF available:* Congress could make the full balance of the FBF available to GSA. GSA would then have resources to provide the full array of services for which it charges agencies, including repairs and alterations. In 2011, we reported that GSA's overall obligational authority has trended downward in recent years, resulting in GSA reducing spending on repairs and alternations and new construction. GSA officials and OMB staff noted that such repairs have the potential to be more expensive if delayed.[34] Making the full balance of the FBF available to GSA would increase funding for GSA to complete projects for agencies, but it would mean less congressional fiscal control and less funding for other mission critical needs. OMB staff noted that with access to all of its receipts, the FBF would be able to meet necessary recapitalization needs, such as major repairs and alterations.

- *Adjust the FBF pricing structure to exclude certain major renovations:* To ensure that the GSA charges cover all services provided under agreements with tenant agencies, GSA could choose to exclude certain major renovations from agreed upon services.[35] GSA could then reduce rents to cover only operations and ongoing maintenance costs of federally-owned buildings. Appropriations decisions to fund capital repairs with rent savings would be made by the agencies' appropriations subcommittees. In effect, this would shift the locus of decision making from GSA's appropriations subcommittee to the appropriations subcommittees of affected agencies. With the change in pricing structure, agencies would have the ability to decide whether to complete funded repairs and alterations in house or use contractors or shared service providers. However, because this option addresses GSA-managed buildings, there may not be an incentive for agencies to carry out this devolution of responsibility amid other priorities and it may be difficult for multi-agency tenant buildings to obtain funding for necessary renovations from their respective appropriations subcommittees. Nevertheless, an agency that uses a GSA-managed building as its headquarters, such as Interior, which has been unable to complete renovations through GSA, would gain some flexibility in completing repairs and alterations by requesting funding directly from its subcommittee. GSA officials noted that separating capital investment funding decisions from operations and maintenance funding decisions could make it difficult to manage the portfolio of government-owned and -leased assets in a strategic manner. They and OMB staff agreed that, without the shared funding aspect of the FBF, it was unlikely that agencies would have sufficient funds available to complete repairs and alterations, even if they were able to maintain the same level of appropriations.
- *Delay recognition of receipts until projects are ready for funding:* To better match FBF receipts with expenses, the recording of receipts from agencies could be held in a temporary account until transferred

to the FBF, temporarily recorded as a mandatory receipt until transferred to the FBF as a discretionary offsetting collection. The receipts would be recorded in the FBF account when funds are appropriated for each "useful asset" of a project. Receipts from agencies to the FBF would then be recorded as discretionary offsets in the fiscal year in which they are appropriated to GSA.

Carve out spending from the discretionary allocations: One approach to further invest in federal real property projects and meet governmentwide priorities could be to allocate resources at the full appropriations committee level, outside the competing priorities of the appropriations subcommittees. The appropriations subcommittees have jurisdiction over different agencies and are responsible for appropriating resources among their relevant agencies. Congress could agree to carve out of the full appropriations committee's 302(a) allocation—the level of spending that the full appropriations committee is authorized to distribute—the amount for federal real property, effectively decreasing the cap for the subcommittees' 302(b) allocations—the level of spending that the subcommittees are authorized to distribute to their respective agencies.[36] This would free up funds for acquiring, disposing of, or repairing and altering space and provide a guaranteed funding level to real property; it would also protect it from competition with other programs that are more focused on spending for consumption activities. In the past, Congress has similarly chosen to allocate resources at the full committee level for certain programs. For example, in 1999 there were five discretionary categories with a separate spending limit "carved out"— violent crime reduction, defense, non-defense, highway, and mass transit.[37] As a result of these carve outs, total spending determinations were made at the full committee level rather than at the subcommittee level.[38]

Carving out of the full committee's allocation spending for federal real property would also "crowd out" spending for all other discretionary programs that might represent a higher priority for the nation. For example, we have previously reported that if a guaranteed minimum funding level for a certain program is carved out of the full committee allocation, and total spending is not increased commensurately, then the remaining activities must compete for the reduced amount that is left.[39] Alternatively, the total cap for the subcommittees' allocation could be increased to dedicate funding to real property projects. The adjustment of the cap could be triggered by the approval of project proposals accompanied by business case analyses.

Related Questions on the Implementation of Discretionary Options:

1. If individual agencies and their respective appropriators and authorizers are responsible for making decisions regarding real property projects, would they have the real property expertise to initiate, implement, fund, authorize, and oversee real property acquisition, repairs/alteration and disposal?
2. If an appropriations carve out for federal real property is made at the full appropriations committee level:
   - How narrowly would those funds be defined? (Deferred maintenance, costs related to preparing properties for disposal)
   - How would a business case analysis be incorporated into obtaining access to carved-out funds?
   - How would the carve out be divided amongst appropriations subcommittees?
   - Might the creation of a Reserve Fund achieve the same purpose?

Mandatory Budget Authority Options Could Increase Agency Flexibility and Improve Cost-Benefit Recognition But Would Require a Different Means of Assuring Fiscal Control

Mandatory budget authority options, such as creating a revolving fund with borrowing authority (e.g., a capital acquisition fund) or a dedicated fund with permanent, indefinite budget authority, could enable the recognition of costs and returns associated with complex real property projects upfront and over time. However, these options would require establishing new account structures and may present different challenges compared to discretionary budget authority options. Existing account structures, such as the Tennessee Valley Authority fund, may provide some insight for policymakers in considering the structure of the revolving fund with borrowing authority or permanent, indefinite budget authority.

Example of a Revolving Fund with Borrowing Authority

The Tennessee Valley Authority fund is an example of a revolving fund with borrowing authority. The fund was created in the Tennessee Valley Authority Act of 1933.

The fund is self-sustaining with revenue earned by supplying electric power to customers in seven states and from exercising its authority to borrow from the public by issuing debt instruments, such as bonds and notes. The fund has a borrowing limit of $30 billion.

Source: GAO analysis of the Tennessee Valley Authority Act of 1933, as amended.

Borrowing authority and permanent, indefinite budget authority could be provided outside of the annual budget and appropriations cycle, allowing for a greater degree of agency flexibility when planning for and carrying out real property projects. Controls on access to funds in both scenarios could be based on comprehensive project proposals with a business case analysis[40] completed by agencies and submitted to the fund manager, OMB and the Congress to ensure their agreement that the project warrants access to this type of funding. This analysis would describe, among other aspects, the nature of the project and potential savings or costs avoided. If the proposal was accepted, funding could be provided for each useful asset. For each useful asset, agencies might provide updated business case analyses, which could include reestimates of both costs and returns.

Borrowing authority is authority granted to a federal entity to borrow funds, then obligate against amounts borrowed. Generally, agencies with borrowing authority are expected to repay the borrowing out of future resources.

Permanent, indefinite budget authority refers to budget authority for an unspecified amount made available as the result of previously enacted legislation and is available without further legislative action. Such budget authority can be the result of substantive legislation or appropriation acts.

Source: GAO-05-734SP.

Mandatory budget authority options may also present opportunities to promote collaboration among agencies with different appropriators and authorizers as well as allow for better alignment of upfront costs with longer-term returns. These options could result in a centralized funding source available to all agencies, which could facilitate consolidation, sharing space, and partnering among agencies for other real property needs. Mandatory options could also be established to receive returns, such as proceeds from disposals, or enforce the recognition of non-monetary returns, such as cost avoidance or cost savings, through revised business case analyses provided by agencies as they complete useful assets of projects. Despite these benefits, mandatory budget authority options could result in a shift of the locus of decision making from appropriators to authorizers, and would create new management and oversight responsibilities for federal entities. In addition, under the pay-as-you-go (PAYGO) budgetary enforcement mechanism, mandatory budget authority options would require costs to be offset by an increase in mandatory receipts or a decrease in mandatory spending for other programs.[41] Nonetheless, these options could result in cost savings and cost avoidance over the long term.

A *capital acquisition fund* (CAF) is a mechanism for financing federal real property projects with the goal of improving decision making by reflecting annual costs in program budgets and helping ameliorate increases in budget authority for projects without forfeiting upfront cost recognition.

Source: GAO-05-249.

Create a capital acquisition fund (CAF): Congress could provide budget authority in the form of borrowing authority to a governmentwide capital acquisition fund (CAF) managed by a single agency, such as GSA.

In contrast to a department-level CAF, which we have previously reported on,[42] a centralized governmentwide CAF could provide funding for real property projects for all agencies. The fund could complement the FBF by providing upfront funding for complex, multi-prospectus level projects or projects estimated to exceed a certain total cost threshold while the FBF could be used for relatively straightforward rental and maintenance expenses. The governmentwide CAF could be subject to a borrowing limit and provide upfront funding for the full cost of projects (or useful assets of projects). As depicted in Figure 4, a governmentwide CAF could be established to:

1. Use its authority to borrow from the Federal Financing Bank (FFB) to fund real property projects agreed upon by Congress, OMB and the CAF manager on a project-by-project basis for all agencies.
2. Use annual payments made by agencies to the CAF to repay the loan from the FFB. The annual payments—provided by agencies' subcommittee appropriators—would be principal and interest amortized over the useful life of the asset, allowing the agency to spread the project cost over time.

3. Automatically receive other monetary returns associated with real property projects to be used for future real property projects or deficit reduction. During implementation as well as at completion of projects, agencies would inform the CAF (along with Congress and OMB) about all returns, including nonmonetary returns, such as cost avoidance or cost savings, via revised business case analyses.

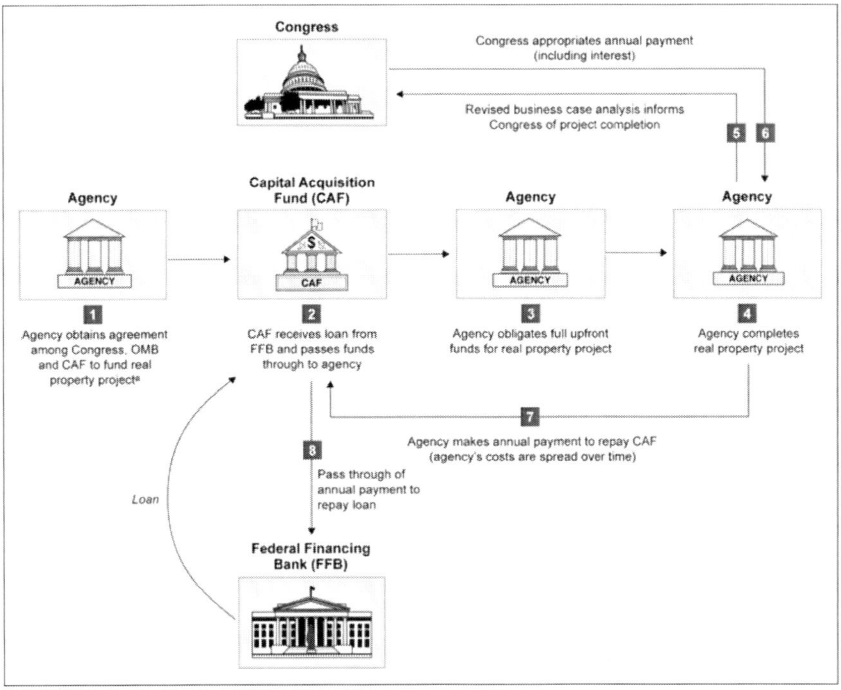

Source; GAO analysis.

Figure 4. One Model for Obtaining Funding Through a Government-wide Capital Acquisition Fund (CAF).

Establish a dedicated fund with permanent, indefinite budget authority: Congress could pass legislation to establish a governmentwide, dedicated fund with permanent, indefinite budget authority instead of borrowing authority. Similar to the CAF, this fund could be managed by a single agency, such as GSA. As depicted in Figure 5, it could automatically receive sums as needed, eliminating the need for annual appropriation to acquire, dispose of, or repair and alter federal real property. The dedicated fund could be at least partially replenished as agencies return net proceeds, such as proceeds from the sale of a building. The fund could complement the FBF by providing upfront funding for complex, multi-prospectus level projects or projects estimated to exceed a certain total cost threshold while the FBF could be used for relatively straightforward rental and maintenance expenses. One concern with providing permanent, indefinite budget authority is that it could reduce agency incentives to provide credible cost estimates in their business case analyses; initial estimates might be artificially low if agencies are held harmless for additional costs that result from price changes.

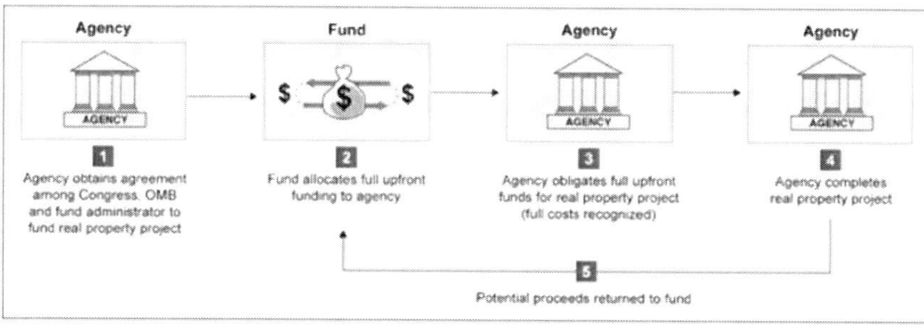

Source: GAO analysis.

Figure 5. One Model for Obtaining Funding Through a Dedicated Fund.

Related Questions on the Implementation of Mandatory Options:

1. What would be the budget enforcement implications for providing permanent, indefinite budget authority and borrowing authority in the mandatory options? Given that federal budgeting rules require that increases in mandatory spending be offset by decreases in other mandatory spending (or an increase in mandatory receipts),[43] where would the offset come from to meet this condition?
2. How narrowly would the use of the mandatory options be defined? For example, would it be meant only for civilian federal real property needs?
3. Would the congressional locus of decision making regarding proposed projects reside with appropriators or authorizers?
4. How would the business case analysis process work? What criteria would be used to consider proposed projects for approval?
5. How would appropriators be involved in the business case analysis process?
6. What mechanisms could be used to ensure that returns are realized in future years?

7. What budget process changes would be needed to ensure that subcommittee appropriators would provide funding to agencies to make annual payments to the CAF to repay the FFB in future years?

Concluding Observations

A central goal of the budget process is to assist the Congress in allocating governmentwide resources efficiently. In the context of federal real property, recognizing costs up front when resource allocation decisions are made is one way to achieve this goal. Given that full upfront funding is an effective way to ensure recognition of commitments embodied in budgeting decisions, an examination of budgetary changes that could improve cost-benefit recognition provides an opportunity to help Congress achieve this goal. Our selected agencies have experienced challenges receiving full upfront funding for federal real property projects through the annual appropriations process and instead have used alternative funding mechanisms, such as public-private partnerships and operating leases to meet long-term needs.

In times of fiscal pressure, employing alternative funding mechanisms to carry out real property projects can appear attractive to agencies because it does not first require obtaining full upfront funding. However, there are inherent risks in using an alternative funding mechanism and many factors affect the outcome. For example, employing alternative funding mechanisms may result in funding federal real property investments without recognizing their true, full costs. This could mean that assets financed through alternative mechanisms may be selected over other equally worthy projects that are competing for full upfront funding. Moreover, with the administration's emphasis on "freezing the footprint," investment decisions that do not recognize costs upfront and returns over time may not result in an appropriate assessment of the size and cost of the federal real property inventory.

We have presented options for alternative budgetary structures that congressional decision makers may wish to consider. Alternative budgetary structures, such as modifying the Federal Buildings Fund (FBF) or establishing a mandatory dedicated fund, could help them recognize a project's full upfront costs and returns over time. While these options could increase flexibility for agencies in addressing their real property needs, they could also result in less fiscal control for Congress. However, if accompanied by appropriate congressional oversight and rigorous financial management, these options may be useful in facilitating prudent real property investment within the current unified budget structure.

There is no single best option, and all options we explored would have considerable challenges that would need to be weighed against potential benefits. In addition, there are broader considerations associated with funding real property projects beyond the scope of this report. Both Congress and agencies have a role in effectively managing real property projects. The authorization or use of an alternative funding mechanism or an alternative budgetary structure requires consideration of tradeoffs to arrive at a deliberate choice that neither creates disincentives for agencies to seek upfront funding nor minimizes fiscal control required by Congress.

We provided a draft of this report for review and comment to the Secretaries of the Departments of Agriculture (USDA), Interior, and Veterans Affairs (VA), and to the Administrator of the General Services Administration (GSA). All agencies generally concurred with our findings. In his written response, the VA Chief of Staff discussed challenges with several of the potential alternative budgetary structures outlined in the report. As we say in our report, while we explored alternative budgetary structure options, each option has both benefits and challenges and we make no recommendations with respect to adopting any of these options. Further, our report states that any potential mandatory alternative budgetary structure to fund large projects would be used by agencies voluntarily, complementing upfront funding through the appropriations process and the Federal Buildings Fund. We further clarified this point in our report. In his written statement, GSA's Administrator expanded upon the challenges that we report agencies experience in funding upfront costs that could lead to long-term savings. He also stated that some of the described alternative budgetary structures would be more effective than others. USDA, Interior, and VA provided technical comments, which we incorporated as appropriate. We also provided a copy of the report to the Office of Management and Budget, which provided technical comments that we incorporated as appropriate.

Sincerely yours,
Susan J. Irving,
Director for Federal Budget Analysis Strategic Issues

End Notes

[1] For example, in 67 General Service Administration (GSA) leases we examined in a series of reports since 1995, the government could have saved almost $1 billion if it had constructed rather than leased space for federal agencies. See GAO, Federal Real Property: Greater Transparency and Strategic Focus Needed for High-Value GSA Leases. GAO-13-744 (Washington, D.C.: Sept. 19, 2013).

[2] We have previously reported on the federal government's use of the unified budget. The unified budget allows the federal government to treat spending on real property projects like any current operating expense. The unified budget recognizes the federal government's involvement in national economic stability and growth, a responsibility that is uniquely federal and requires the government to focus on total spending in relation to total revenue. Reforms in how the federal government budgets for real property projects should be considered, but any capital budgeting allocation process should be studied within the overall constraints of a fiscal policy based on unified budget principles. See GAO, Budget Issues: Budgeting for Capital, GAO/T-AIMD-98-99 (Washington, D.C.: Mar. 6, 1998) and Pros and Cons of a Separate Capital Budget for the Federal Government. GAO/PAD-83-1 (Washington, D.C.: Sept 22, 1983).

[3] For agencies with the largest federal real property holdings, see GAO, Federal Real Property: Strategic Partnerships and Local Coordination Could Help Agencies Better Utilize Space, GAO-12-779 (Washington, D.C.: July 25, 2012). We have previously reported that while sound data collection practices in designing and maintaining the Federal Real Property Profile database have not been followed, the Federal Real Property Profile can be used in a general sense to track assets. See GAO, Federal Real Property: National Strategy and Better Data Needed to Improve Management of Excess and Underutilized Property, GAO-12-645 (Washington, D.C.: June 20, 2012).

[4] GAO, Budget Issues: Alternative Approaches to Finance Federal Capital, GAO-03-1011 (Washington, D.C.: Aug. 21, 2003).

[5] Memorandum—Disposing of Unneeded Federal Real Estate—Increasing Sale Proceeds, Cutting Operations Costs, and Improving Energy Efficiency, 75 Fed. Reg. 33987 (June 16, 2010). We have previously reported on agencies' reported cost savings in response to the June 2010 memorandum. GAO, Federal Real Property: Improved Standards Needed to Ensure That Agencies' Reported Cost Savings Are Reliable and Transparent. GAO-14-12 (Washington, D.C.: Oct. 29, 2013)

[6] Letter from Jacob J. Lew, Director, Office of Management and Budget, to The Honorable Joseph R. Biden, President of the Senate (May 4, 2011)

[7] The Government Performance and Results Modernization Act requires in part that the federal government set cross-agency priority goals which are outcome-oriented and improve management across the federal government in areas of information technology, financial management, human resources, and real property. Pub. L. No. 111-352, § 5, 124 Stat. 3873 (Jan. 4, 2011).

[8] These stakeholders include state and local governments, business interests in the communities where the real property assets are located, private sector construction and leasing firms, historic preservation organizations, various advocacy groups, and the public in general, which often views the facilities as the physical face of the federal government in their communities. At both the national and local levels, federal real property practices also often attract significant media attention, particularly when these practices are under scrutiny for waste and mismanagement. See GAO, Federal Real Property: Progress made Toward

Addressing Problems, but Underlying Obstacles Continue to Hamper Reform. GAO-07-349 (Washington, D.C.: April 13, 2007).

[9] A useful asset is an economically and programmatically separate segment of procuring an asset or whole asset. The total asset procurement may include one or more useful assets. Preparation, Submission, and Execution of the Budget, app. J OMB Circular No. A-11 (2013).

[10] See GAO, Understanding Similarities and Differences between Accrual and Cash Deficits, GAO-07-117SP (Washington, D.C.: December 2006).

[11] When capital assets are purchased, the budget recognizes the full cost up front to provide decision-makers with the information and incentives to make efficient decisions at the only time that they can control the cost. However, under the accrual basis of accounting used in the financial statements, the cost of the asset is initially recorded on the balance sheet. The cost of the asset is then spread over its expected useful life to match the asset's cost with its use.

[12] For operating leases funded by GSA's FBF, which is self-insuring under existing authority, only the amount of budget authority needed to cover the annual lease payment is required to be obligated.

[13] GSA appraises its inventory on a 5 year cycle—approximately 20 percent of its owned inventory annually—and charges rent based on rates for comparable assets in the private sector. GSA charges its tenants in space leased from the private sector rates equal to the cost of the lease plus either a 7 percent (for cancelable assignments) or 5 percent (for noncancelable assignments) administrative fee to cover its management costs.

[14] American Recovery and Reinvestment Act of 2009, Pub. L. No. 111-5, div. A, title V, 123 Stat. 115, 149 (Feb. 17, 2009)

[15] GSA continues to include the results of an alternatives analysis in its prospectuses for capital construction and renovation projects but does not do so in its prospectuses for leases. See GAO-13-744.

[16] See GAO-13-744.

[17] In past work, we have found that GSA relies heavily on high-priced operating leases to meet new long-term needs because it typically lacks the upfront funding needed to purchase buildings or space. For example, in 2007, we reported that although building ownership options through construction or purchase are generally the least expensive ways to meet agencies' long-term space needs, GSA relied heavily on operating leases to meet new long-term needs because it lacked funds to pursue ownership. See GAO-13-744 and GAO, Federal Real Property: Progress Made Towards Addressing Problems, but Underlying Obstacles Continue to Hamper Reform, GAO-07-349 (Washington, D.C.: Apr.13, 2007.)

[18] Columbia Plaza's close proximity to State's headquarters building makes it a desirable office space for State's purposes. GSA has leased space in Columbia Plaza since 1974.

[19] GSA officials stated that while a purchase option as part of a lease agreement can be advantageous in the right circumstances, GSA carefully considers its inclusion when negotiating a contract because a purchase option often includes a premium factored into the terms of the lease.

[20] See GAO, Federal Buildings Fund: Improved Transparency and Long-term Plan Needed to Clarify Capital Funding Priorities, GAO-12-646 (Washington, D.C.: July 12, 2012).

[21] Obligational authority includes adjustments due to reprogramming and rescissions.

[22] Forest Service Facility Realignment and Enhancement Act of 2005, Pub. L. No. 109-54, title V, §505, 119 Stat. 499,563 (Aug. 2, 2005).

[23] GAO has done previous work on VA's use of EULs to redevelop underutilized federal real property. For more information, see GAO, Federal Real Property: Improved Cost Reporting Would Help Decision Makers Weigh the Benefits of Enhanced Use Leasing. GAO-13-14 (Washington, D.C.: Dec. 19, 2012).

[24] Officials reported historic status, stakeholder interest, and legal authorities are challenges to disposing of or demolishing buildings.

[25] Honoring America's Veterans and Caring for Camp Lejeune Families Act of 2012, Pub. L. No. 112-154, title II, § 211, 126 Stat. 1165, 1179-1180 (Aug. 6, 2012).

[26] See GAO, Congressionally Chartered Organizations: Key Principles for Leveraging Nonfederal Resources, GAO-13-549 (Washington, D.C.: June. 7, 2013).

[27] See GAO-13-549.

[28] See GAO-13-549.

[29] We have previously reported on the federal government's use of the unified budget. Within the unified budget, the federal government treats spending on real property projects like any current operating expense. The unified budget recognizes the federal government's involvement in national economic stability and growth, a responsibility that is uniquely federal and requires the government to focus on total spending in relation to total revenue. Reforms in how the federal government budgets for real property projects should be considered, but any capital budgeting allocation process should be studied within the overall constraints of a fiscal policy based on unified budget principles. See GAO GAO/PAD-83-1 and GAO/T-AIMD-98-99.

[30] National infrastructure banks have been proposed to provide funding for broad infrastructure needs through an independent entity that could provide credit to support qualified infrastructure projects, such as transportation, water, and energy infrastructure primarily owned by state and local governments and the private sector. Because this report focuses on federally-owned real property, we do not address national infrastructure banks.

[31] 40 U.S.C. § 3307.

[32] See GAO, Executive Guide: Leading Practices in Capital Decision-Making, GAO/AIMD-99-32 (Washington, D.C.: December 1998) and GAO, Federal Capital: Three Entities' Implementation of Capital Planning Principles Is Mixed, GAO-07-274 (Washington, D.C.: February 23, 2007).

[33] Obligational authority includes adjustments due to reprogramming and rescissions.

[34] See GAO, Federal Buildings Fund: Improved Transparency and Long-Term Plan Needed to Clarify Capital Funding Priorities, GAO-12-646 (Washington, D.C.: July 12, 2012).

[35] As previously described, repairs, alterations and new construction are the most affected by GSA's lack of access to the full balance of the FBF.

[36] Section 302(a) of the Congressional Budget and Impoundment Control Act of 1974 stipulates that an allocation is the distribution of spending authority and outlays to relevant committees, based on levels contained in budget resolutions. This is known as the full committee's allocation. Section 302(b) stipulates that an allocation is the distribution of spending and outlay authorities to relevant subcommittees based on the levels contained in a budget resolution. This is known as the subcommittee allocation. Pub. L. No. 93-344, 88 Stat.297 (July 12, 1974).

[37] See GAO, Budget Issues: Cap Structure and Guaranteed Funding, GAO/T-AIMD-99-210 (Washington, D.C.: July 21, 1999).

[38] In the past, these spending limits served as a cap, not a floor; thus less than the capped amount could be appropriated, but any unused portion could not be reallocated to other areas of the budget.

[39] See GAO/T-AIMD-99-210.

[40] Business case analyses might include such things as how the project aligns with the agency's strategic plan, needs assessment and gap identification, alternatives evaluations, life-cycle costs, a schedule of project milestones and deliverables, and cost-benefit analyses. See GAO, Executive Guide: Leading Practices in Decision-Making, GAO/AIMD-99-32 (Washington, D.C.: December 1998) and GAO, Federal Capital: Three Entities' Implementation of Capital Planning Principles Is Mixed, GAO-07-274 (Washington, D.C.: Feb. 23, 2007).

[41] Under PAYGO, proposed changes in, or new permanent, law may not increase the deficit. Budget Enforcement Act of 1990 Pub. L. No. 101-508, 104 Stat. 1388 (Nov. 5, 1990), as amended by Statutory Pay-As-You-Go Act of 2010, Pub. L. No. 111-139, 124 Stat. 8 (Feb. 12, 2010).

[42] We previously reported that establishing a department-level CAF would be a complex process and the benefits of such a structure could be achieved through simpler means. A department-level CAF would use borrowing authority to buy new departmental subunit assets. The subunits would then pay the CAF a mortgage payment, which the CAF would use to pay back the loan from the Treasury. For more information, see GAO, Capital Financing: Potential Benefits of Capital Acquisition Funds Can Be Achieved through Simpler Means, GAO-05-249 (Washington, D.C.: April 8, 2005).

[43] 2 U.S.C. §§ 931-939.

In: Federal Real Property: Analyses of Key Issues ISBN: 978-1-63482-278-7
Editor: Adam B. Clark

Chapter 3

OVERSEAS REAL PROPERTY: STATE DEPARTMENT NEEDS TO IMPROVE GUIDANCE AND RECORDS MANAGEMENT*

United States Government Accountability Office

ABBREVIATIONS

ACT	Foreign Buildings Act
CSCS	Capital Security Cost Sharing
DOD	Department of Defense
FAM	*Foreign Affairs Manual*
FRPP	Federal Real Property Profile
IG	Inspector General
NEC	new embassy compound
OBO	Bureau of Overseas Buildings Operations
OMB	Office of Management and Budget
STATE	U.S. Department of State

* This is an edited, reformatted and augmented version of The United States Government Accountability Office publication, GAO-14-769, dated September 2014.

Why GAO Did This Study

The Department of State (State) holds or leases about 70-million square feet of real estate in about 275 posts worldwide and has the authority to construct, acquire, manage, and dispose of real property abroad.

GAO was asked to review State's management of overseas real property. This report examines: (1) what is known about State's overseas real property inventory, and (2) what factors State considers in managing its overseas real property portfolio and to what extent it documents its decision-making process pertaining to real property.

GAO requested 202 files for all acquisitions, disposals, and major leases pertaining to State's management of its real property abroad for the period from 2008-2013. In addition, GAO interviewed State officials in headquarters and at four posts abroad, selected because they had (1) ongoing or recently completed embassy construction or renovation projects without property disposals, (2) properties reported as identified for disposal for multiple years without being disposed, and (3) both owned and leased properties. The results of the four case studies cannot be generalized for the purpose of this review.

What GAO Recommends

GAO recommends that the Secretary of State (1) clarify accounting code guidance for tracking expenses related to disposal of unneeded properties, and (2) take steps to collect and retain documents related to real property purchases, disposals, and leases in accordance with the *FAM* and OMB's guidance. State concurred with GAO's recommendations.

What GAO Found

GAO's analysis of the overseas real property portfolio of the Department of State (State) indicates that the overall inventory has increased in recent years. State reported that its leased properties, which make up about 75 percent of its inventory, increased from approximately 12,000 to 14,000 between 2008 and 2013. State's numbers of federally owned properties increased, but comparing the total number of owned properties from year to year can be misleading because State's method of counting these properties has been evolving over the past several years. Specifically, according to State officials, they have been revising their method for counting properties to produce more precise counts and to meet reporting guidance from the Office of Management and Budget (OMB), among others. For example, State began counting separately structural assets previously included as part of another building's assets, such as guard booths or perimeter walls, and consequently reported approximately 650 additional structural assets in fiscal year 2012 than in 2011, and approximately 900 more structures in 2013.

State officials told GAO that they consider many factors in managing real property; however, GAO found State's available data and documentation on management decisions were limited. State officials said that they work with overseas posts to identify and dispose of unneeded properties, primarily using factors in State's *Foreign Affairs Manual* (*FAM*) guidance. Such factors include identifying properties deemed obsolete or with excessive maintenance costs. State collects data on costs associated with unneeded properties identified for disposal, relying on posts to charge all such costs to a specific accounting code. The four posts GAO visited did not use this code consistently. For example, officials at one post charged some disposal costs to a routine maintenance account. Officials at the other posts with properties for sale used the code to charge all related disposal costs. GAO also found that other posts with unneeded properties identified for disposal in fiscal year 2013 had not charged expenses to this account. The guidance provided in the *FAM* for using this code does not detail the types of costs that can be charged. This omission raises questions about the extent to which posts use the code as State intends and the extent to which State receives accurate and comprehensive cost information about its unneeded properties. State, without accurate data on unneeded property, may not have the information it needs to make a decision about property offers when attempting to maximize revenue for property sales. Also, posts may not have sufficient funding for routine property maintenance if they use funds designated for this type of maintenance on unneeded property. GAO requested to review 202 files between fiscal year 2008 through 2013 on acquisitions (72), disposals (94), and leases (36), but was provided 90, as State told GAO that these files were not centrally located and too time consuming to find and provide during the time frame of our review. State provided most of what it considers "core" documents for the acquisition and disposal files, but these documents do not constitute all of the documentation listed in the *FAM* and OMB guidance. In addition, although State provided all 36 of the requested lease files, some documentation that State agreed to provide was missing for 30 of the 36 files. Without the missing files and documentation, it is unclear how efficiently and effectively State is managing its overseas real property.

* * *

September 25, 2014

The Honorable Edward R. Royce
Chairman

The Honorable Eliot L. Engel
Ranking Member
Committee on Foreign Affairs
House of Representatives

The U.S. government, through the U.S. Department of State (State), owns or leases approximately 70-million square feet of real estate in approximately 275 posts worldwide. These properties include embassies, consulates, office space, warehouses, and housing for U.S. diplomatic staff. In addition, State currently has $7.5 billion in projects to design and construct new facilities. This new construction will gradually replace vulnerable embassy facilities around the world. It may also result in potential revenue from the disposal of property vacated as personnel move into newly constructed facilities and savings as leases expire or State terminates unneeded leases. State is authorized to retain and reinvest the proceeds from foreign property disposals into United States government property acquisitions or other authorized purposes.

In our previous reports on State's real property, we have found problems such as inaccuracies with its real-property inventory database, problems that hindered State's ability to identify and dispose of properties that were unneeded or expensive to maintain, and that could produce millions of dollars in revenue for the U.S. government.[1] By implementing recommendations made in our 2002 report, State identified and sold unneeded properties resulting in nearly $756 million in proceeds.[2] Furthermore, we have identified real property as high risk government-wide, and since State has an expansive construction program, it is important that it manage its real property in ways to ensure efficient use of resources.[3] Given this importance, you asked us to review State's management of real property. Specifically, in this report we examine: 1) what is known about State's overseas real-property inventory, and

2) what factors State considers in managing its overseas real-property portfolio and to what extent it documents its decision-making process.

We took several steps to address these objectives. Specifically, to understand what is known about State's real property portfolio and how State reports real property data, we obtained and reviewed State's Federal Real Property Profile (FRPP) data from fiscal years 2008 through 2013, which State reports to the General Services Administration yearly. Additionally, we reviewed State's real property reports to Congress and compared these reports with State's annual FRPP submissions to determine differences in reported real property between these reports. We determined that FRPP data were sufficiently reliable for the purpose of reporting approximate numbers of properties in State's portfolio, by interviewing knowledgeable Bureau of Overseas Buildings Operations (OBO) and post officials about data quality-assurance procedures and reviewing related documentation, including previous State Inspector General (IG) reports, our prior work, data dictionaries and user manuals, and data verification practices. We also reviewed State's internal report on costs associated with properties identified for disposal to determine costs for unneeded properties that State is selling and found that the data had limitations, which we discuss later in this report.

To determine the extent to which State documents its decision-making process, we requested documentation from State's real property disposals, acquisitions, and leases from fiscal years 2008 through 2013. Specifically, we requested files on 202 properties. This request included all 94 property disposals reported to Congress during this period, of which State provided 20. We requested files on all 72 property acquisitions that State reported to Congress during this period, of which State provided 34.[4]

We also requested, and were provided, all 36 major leases with $500,000 or more in annual rent, as defined in State's *Foreign Affairs Manual* (*FAM*) that were active from fiscal years 2008 through 2013 and still were listed as active in FRPP at the end of fiscal year 2013.[5] We compared State's documentation of the disposals, acquisitions, and leases to the documentation specifications in *FAM* and Office of Management and Budget (OMB) circulars. Also, we obtained information on how State reinvested revenue generated from property disposals between fiscal years 2008 through 2013. We reviewed this information and determined that it was sufficiently reliable for our purposes by interviewing knowledgeable officials and corroborating the data with information reported to Congress.

To gather information on factors State considers in managing its real property portfolio, we interviewed State Department officials at OBO and at four selected posts (Belgrade, Serbia; Helsinki, Finland; London, United Kingdom; and Sarajevo, Bosnia and Herzegovina). We selected these posts because they had (1) ongoing or recently completed embassy construction or renovation projects without disposing of properties, (2) properties reported as identified for disposal for multiple years without being disposed of, and (3) a mix of owned and leased properties. We based our site-visit selection on these factors in order to observe posts with (1) higher numbers of property disposals than other posts due to recently completed or ongoing construction of new embassies, (2) persistent challenges in selling unneeded properties, and (3) experience managing both owned and leased properties. The results of the case studies provide insight into State's management and decision-making practices but cannot be generalized for the purposes of this review.

We conducted this performance audit from June 2013 to September 2014 in accordance with generally accepted government auditing standards. Those standards require that we plan and perform the audit to obtain sufficient, appropriate evidence to provide a reasonable basis for our findings and conclusions based on our audit objectives. We believe that the evidence obtained provides a reasonable basis for our findings and conclusions based on our audit objectives. Further details on our scope and methodology can be found in appendix I.

BACKGROUND

State has authority to acquire, manage, and dispose of real property abroad. Specifically, the Foreign Buildings Act (Act) of 1926, as amended, authorizes the Secretary of State to acquire by purchase, construction, exchange, or lease sites and buildings in foreign cities for use by diplomatic and consular establishments of the United States.[6] The Act allows State to alter, repair, furnish, and dispose of these properties, and to provide residential and office space and necessary related facilities to federal agencies abroad. It also authorizes the Secretary to apply disposal proceeds toward real property needs or to deposit proceeds into the Foreign Service Buildings Fund and use the proceeds for authorized purposes.

OBO manages State's real property abroad to support U.S. government presence at embassies and consulates, which are also known as missions or posts. This office is responsible for managing U.S. government-owned and government-leased real property, which includes land, structures, and buildings such as embassies, warehouses, offices, and residences. OBO coordinates directly with officials at posts tasked with managing the post's real property. Posts are responsible for implementing OBO policies related to the management, acquisition, disposal, and reporting of real property, outlined in State's *FAM*. Table 1 below provides an overview of OBO's and the posts' roles and responsibilities for real property management.

Table 1. Department of State Overseas Real Property Management Roles and Responsibilities

	Responsibilities	
Activity	Overseas Buildings Operations (OBO)	Overseas posts
Acquisitions	Identify markets with high returns on investment and work with posts to select properties to acquire; obtain independent fair market value appraisal(s), and hire brokers, if needed to assist.	Prepare and submit acquisition proposal to OBO; select legal expert and surveyor for title investigation, survey, pre-and post-purchase certifications.
Disposals	Approve or deny disposal requests from posts; obtain two independent appraisal(s); hire brokers to market properties.	Review owned and capital lease properties annually to identify and report to OBO any properties that are unneeded, underutilized, or uneconomical to retain; submit disposal request to OBO.
Leasing	Set leasing-cost targets for posts and review waiver requests for leases that exceed size and/or cost standards. Obtain an independent appraisal on functional leases with annual rents exceeding $250,000, residential leases with annual rents exceeding $120,000 per year, and all designated residences meeting certain criteria.	Identify potential residential properties for lease, contact landlord, and negotiate lease terms according to guidance and lease template provided in Foreign Affairs Manual.
Reporting	Input information on owned and capital lease properties into State's real property database. Prepare and submit State's annual Federal Real Property Profile report to the General Services Administration. Submit real property reports to Congress.	Input information about operating leases into State's realproperty database. The Chief of Mission at each post verifies the accuracy of all reported data in annual statement to OBO.

Source: GAO summary of Department of State Foreign Affairs Manual and additional information provided by State. | GAO-14-769.

In 2004, the administration added managing federal real property to the President's Management Agenda and the President issued an executive order directing executive agencies to submit real property information annually for inclusion in a single, comprehensive database, which is now known as the Federal Real Property Profile (FRPP) that provides an annual report on the government's real property holdings.[7]

State is currently undertaking a multiyear, multibillion-dollar capital-security construction program to replace 214 of its facilities abroad due to security concerns. State is taking these steps due to continuing threats and incidences such as the terrorist bombings in 1998 of embassies in Dar es Salaam, Tanzania, and Nairobi, Kenya, that killed more than 220 people and injured 4,000 others. The program incorporates the requirements of the Secure Embassy Counterterrorism Act of 1999 and instructs State to replace facilities at vulnerable posts and to require that all new diplomatic facilities be sufficiently sized to ensure that all U.S. government personnel at the post work onsite.[8] Construction projects are prioritized by State's annual risk matrix that ranks facilities based on their vulnerability across a wide range of security threats. In 2004, to aid in the construction of new embassies, a related program, the Capital Security Cost Sharing (CSCS) program was authorized, which required agencies with personnel overseas to provide funding for the construction of new, secure, and safe diplomatic facilities for U.S. government personnel overseas.[9] State expects funding of $2.2 billion per year over a 5 year period through fiscal year 2018 to carry out new construction projects.

STATE'S OVERSEAS REAL PROPERTY INVENTORY HAS INCREASED, BUT DATA DO NOT ALLOW FOR COMPARISONS ACROSS YEARS

Our analysis of State's real property portfolio indicated that the overall inventory has increased. State reported its leased properties, which make up approximately 75 percent of the inventory, increased from approximately 12,000 to 14,000 between 2008 and 2013.[10] However, comparing the total number of owned properties between years can be misleading because State's method of counting these properties has been evolving over the past several years. OBO officials explained that in response to changes in OMB's and FRPP's reporting guidance, they have made efforts to count properties more precisely. For example, OBO has focused on separately capturing structural assets previously recorded as part of another building asset, such as perimeter walls, guard booths, and other ancillary structures. As a result of this effort,

State recorded approximately 650 additional structural assets in its fiscal year 2012 FRPP report and approximately 900 more structures the following year in its fiscal year 2013 FRPP report, according to OBO officials. Additionally, OBO officials told us that former Department of Defense (DOD) properties in Iraq and Afghanistan were transferred to State; the largest of these transfers occurred in 2012 when State assumed responsibility from DOD for approximately 400 properties in Iraq. State reported additional changes in its real property portfolio, which are described below.

Acquisitions: State reported spending more than $600 million to acquire nearly 300 properties from fiscal year 2008 through 2013 (see fig.1).[11] State uses two sources of funding to acquire real property. It acquires land for building new embassy compounds (NEC) with funding from the CSCS program. It acquires residences, offices, and other functional facilities with proceeds from the disposal of unneeded property. In fiscal years 2008 through 2013, State reported spending approximately $400 million of these disposal proceeds to acquire approximately 230 properties.

Disposals: From fiscal years 2008 through 2013, State reported selling approximately 170 properties. In doing so, it received approximately $695 million in proceeds (see fig.1). According to State, property vacated when personnel move into newly constructed facilities is the largest source of property that can be disposed of. When State completes construction of a NEC, personnel previously working in different facilities at multiple locations are then collocated into the same NEC, a move that provides State an opportunity to dispose of its former facilities. Further information on State's acquisitions and disposals from fiscal year 2008 through 2013, can be found in figures 1 and 2 below.

Leases: The majority of State's leased properties are residences. State reported spending approximately $500 million on leases in 2013 and projects a potential increase to approximately $550 million by 2016 as growing populations in urban centers around the world push rental costs higher and the U.S. government's overseas presence increases.

OBO provides guidance to posts for disposing of unneeded properties as the post prepares to move into a NEC. In Belgrade, OBO is working with the post to sell an old embassy that is no longer needed following the completion of Belgrade's NEC. Post officials told us that relocating to the NEC in April 2013 allowed them to market their old embassy and terminate multiple leases.

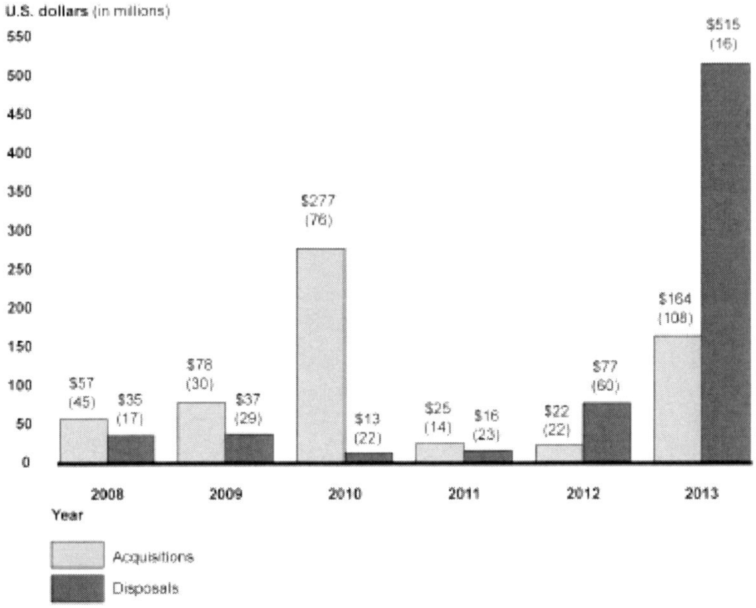

Source: GAO analysis of Department of State information. | GAO-14-769.

Notes: The numbers of properties are in parentheses. Dollars are not adjusted for inflation. The relatively large increases in acquisitions in fiscal years 2010 and 2013 are due to the acquisition of land for a new London embassy ($183 million) in 2010 and an office building in Paris ($55 million) in 2013. The increase in fiscal year 2013 disposals is due to the sale of the current London embassy ($437 million). The new London embassy is currently under construction with completion expected in 2017.

Figure 1. Department of State Overseas Real Property Acquisitions and Disposals, Fiscal Years 2008 through 2013.

In London, State sold its existing embassy building in August 2013 to fund the construction of a NEC. State is leasing the existing building until construction of the NEC is completed, which is expected in 2017.

NEC construction has also provided State the opportunity to sell residential properties that are not located near the new embassies under construction. For example, according to post officials in London, transitioning to the NEC in London allowed State to make cost effective changes in its residential property portfolio by selling valuable older properties near the current embassy and purchasing newer lower cost residences near the NEC.

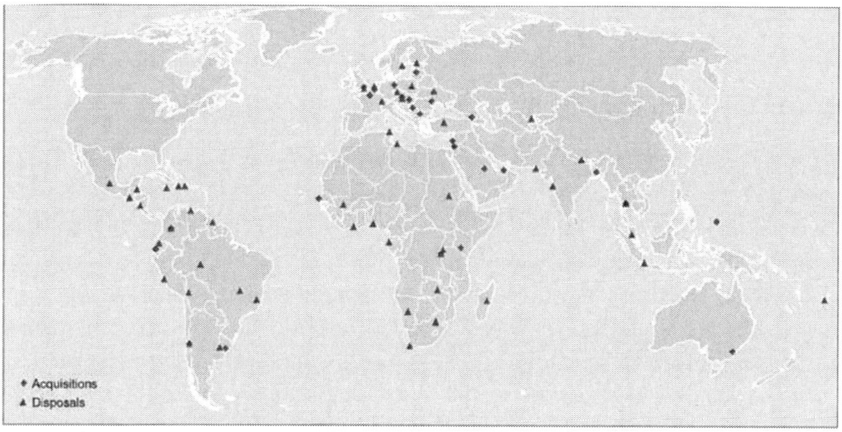

Source: GAO analysis of Department of State information. | GAO-14-769.
Note: This map illustrates acquisitions and disposals reported in the Department of State's asset management account.

Figure 2. Map of Department of State Acquisitions and Disposals, Fiscal Years 2008 through 2013.

State reports these types of real property transactions to Congress quarterly. Also, as required, State submits annual reports to Congress listing surplus overseas properties that have been identified for sale.[12] For example, our analysis found that State listed 39 properties that it identified for disposal in its fiscal year 2013 annual report to Congress. Some properties identified as unneeded in State's fiscal year 2013 FRPP report were not included in the 2013 annual report to Congress, such as a former embassy in Tashkent, Uzbekistan; land in New Delhi, India, and Manila, Philippines; and various properties in Beijing, China. According to OBO officials, the annual reports to Congress do not include unneeded properties they expect to retain or have determined they cannot sell for various reasons, such as host government restrictions related to diplomatic or political differences. For example, according to a State IG report, after State refused to pay what it considered an illegal tax to support the Brazilian social security system in 1996, the government of Brazil blocked the disposal of all U.S. diplomatic properties in the country.[13] OBO officials told us that they do not report unneeded properties that cannot be sold because the Congressional reporting requirement is to list surplus properties that have been identified for sale.

State Officials Said That They Consider Many Factors in Managing Their Overseas Real Property, but Data and Documentation Are Limited

State's officials said that they consider many factors in managing their real property portfolio, specifically in terms of identifying and disposing of unneeded property, as well as in purchasing and leasing property. The officials also described challenges associated with each of those aspects of managing the real property portfolio. State collects data on costs associated with properties identified for disposal to track costs, but we found that posts did not use the required code to track these costs consistently. As a result, this raises questions about the extent to which posts worldwide are using the code as State intends, and the extent to which State is receiving accurate and comprehensive cost information about its properties. We requested to review 202 files from fiscal year 2008 through 2013 on acquisitions, disposals, and leases, but were only provided 90 files since, according to State officials, the files were not centrally located and too time consuming to find and provide within the time frame of our review. State was able to provide most of the "core" documents agreed to, although some of the documentation was missing for the 90 files provided. For example, State provided all 36 of the requested lease files, but some documentation that *FAM* and OMB directs State to retain, and that State agreed to provide, was missing for 30 of the 36 lease files provided.

State Considers Various Factors in Identifying Unneeded Property, but Faces Challenges in Disposing of Properties

OBO officials told us that they work with posts to identify and dispose of unneeded properties primarily using factors outlined in *FAM*, along with other strategies. *FAM* lists 18 factors that OBO and posts might consider when identifying and disposing of property (see table 2), such as whether (1) the property has excessive operating costs, (2) State used the property only irregularly, or (3) the property is uneconomical to retain. Officials at two of the four posts we visited told us that they were aware of and use the guidelines to identify unneeded property.[14]

Table 2 Guidance in Department of State's Foreign Affairs Manual on 18 Factors Posts Will Consider in Identifying Unneeded Real Property

1. Is the property wholly or partly excess to needs? If so, could it be sold, licensed, leased, or exchanged for more useful property?
2. Is the property uneconomical to retain? If so, could it be sold or exchanged for a more suitable property with lower maintenance and operating costs, at a price roughly equivalent to the value of the present property? Could it be leased or licensed, and other property acquired to meet post needs?
3. Is the property being put to optimum use?
4. Is the property used only irregularly for program purposes? Would a portion of the property satisfy program needs?
5. Have local conditions changed significantly since the property was acquired, thereby affecting the surrounding neighborhood, transportation facilities, convenience to users, zoning, and other environmental factors, including local development plans?
6. Can continued U.S. Government ownership of the property be justified in light of its current use?
7. Are operating and maintenance costs excessive?
8. Is the property functionally obsolete or has it physically deteriorated beyond economical repair?
9. Will program changes alter post property requirements?
10. If a portion of the property is disposed of, will the remaining portion still comply with zoning requirements?
11. Considering property prices or rentals, moving costs, preparation of the new space, occupancy costs, and increased operationalefficiency: Can the U.S. Government realize net savings by relocating?
12. Is a portion of any property being retained primarily because the present boundaries are marked by the existence of fences, hedges, roads, or utilities?
13. Is land being retained only because it is landlocked?
14. Is there land that can be made available for use by others, within or outside the U.S. Government, on a temporary lease or license basis?
15. Are there security, political, or public relations considerations that outweigh the foregoing guidelines?
16. What effect does the availability of alternative facilities, if required, have on the foregoing *guidelines*?
17. Are there any restrictions on the use or expatriation of proceeds of sale under local law?
18. Does the building meet fire and life safety codes and standards?

Source: Department of State, Foreign Affairs Manual (FAM), 15 FAM Exhibit 512.1. | GAO-14-769.

Officials at a third post that owned property was unaware of the guidelines, but told us they used excessive maintenance costs to identify properties for disposal. Excessive maintenance cost is one of the 18 listed factors in *FAM*. OBO also uses other strategies to help identify unneeded property, such as: (1) reviewing the Department's internal property database to identify properties newly classified by posts as unneeded, (2) monitoring new construction to identify property vacated as personnel move to new facilities, (3) reviewing reports of State's (IG) for recommendations on disposals, and (4) evaluating changing political conditions and evolving post conditions to help right-size a post's real estate portfolio.

Once posts identify and OBO approves a property as unneeded, OBO takes the lead in disposing of the property. For example, OBO sold residences in London in fiscal year 2012 and an embassy in fiscal year 2013 (see fig.3), and the Department received approximately $497 million in proceeds that State is using to design and build the new London embassy and to obtain replacement residences closer to the new embassy (see fig.4).[15] OBO also sold a residence in Helsinki in fiscal year 2011 and received approximately $657,000 that was deposited back into its asset management account for other real property needs worldwide.

Source: Elizabeth Gill Lui.| GAO-14-769.

Figure 3. Current London Embassy.

Source: State Department (Photo). © Kleran Timberlake (artist rendering). | GAO-14-769.

Figure 4. Construction Site and Artist Rendering of Future London Embassy.

OBO officials acknowledged challenges with disposing of unneeded properties. These challenges included: the condition and location of facilities, changing missions in countries, and diplomatic reasons or political situations that require State to retain property previously marked as unneeded. For example, unneeded residential units can be in poor condition, which makes selling them challenging. Also, officials told us that the State's primary mission of diplomacy overrides property disposal. In countries such as Mexico, Brazil, and India, policy changes with the diplomatic mission have led to retaining property previously marked as unneeded. For example, in Ciudad Juarez, Mexico, a new consulate was built; however, State retained property to accommodate and expand their mission.

Officials at the posts we visited also described some past and recurring challenges to disposing of unneeded real property:

Officials at the Helsinki and Sarajevo posts told us that differing opinions between OBO and posts about whether to dispose or retain unneeded property presented challenges. For example, officials in Helsinki told us they wanted to dispose of two unneeded residential properties in 2014 because of excessive maintenance costs and a longer commuting time due to the need to take mass transit because parking space was eliminated at the renovated embassy (see fig. 5). However, OBO officials told the post to retain and assign staff to the two properties for an additional 3 years. OBO believed that marketing the two properties, located next to two additional unneeded properties they had been attempting to sell since 2011, would possibly depress the disposal price if all the properties were marketed at the same time. However, post officials believe it will cost the post and State more in maintenance costs to bring the properties to a state of good repair, and believe selling the properties now would be more financially beneficial than retaining the properties for an additional 3 years as the costs to maintain the property would outweigh the potential for increased proceeds.

Source: GAO.| GAO-14-769.

Figure 5. Unneeded Residential Properties in Helsinki.

OBO officials told us that they conduct an internal review to determine the financial benefit of whether to retain or sell properties in these situations as the agency attempts to maximize the disposal value of property. Officials at the Sarajevo post told us that they have had ongoing discussions with OBO about retaining their old embassy and converting it to a new Ambassador's residence. Post officials told us that OBO originally wanted the post to dispose of its interest in the embassy—which State has been leasing for only $1 per year since 1994 with the option to continue the lease at this rate for 150 years. OBO officials told us that, at this below-market lease rate of $1 per year, they anticipated that the disposal of this leasehold interest could generate proceeds for State. However, OBO and post officials told us that the host government denied the Department's request to transfer the lease to a third party. Given the Department's inability to transfer or sell its interest in the property, OBO and the post reached an agreement to retain the embassy and convert it into an Ambassador's residence. When the conversion is complete the post will terminate the lease for its current Ambassador's residence, which has an annual lease cost of $144,000.

- Officials at the Helsinki and Belgrade posts told us that OBO's process for appraising and marketing properties for sale was a challenge in disposing properties in a timely manner. Specifically, the post officials thought OBO's real estate firm's appraisals were too high and made the properties unsellable. OBO acknowledged that ensuring an accurate appraisal price presents challenges and therefore, it also reviews appraisals internally. Also, post officials in Helsinki and Belgrade told us that the global real estate firms OBO hired to market their properties did not have local offices, and thus may have not fully understood the local real estate market. For example, Belgrade post officials told us that an affiliate office in Hungary was marketing their old embassy, and that a Hungarian phone number was the primary number used to market the property, which they believe made selling the property more challenging (see fig. 6).[16] OBO officials told us that they believe the global firms they contract with are more experienced than many local firms.
- Officials at the Belgrade post told us about zoning challenges with the host government that have delayed the disposal of their old embassy. They told us OBO notified the post that it would sell the old embassy once the new embassy had been built. However, post officials told us they have had to resolve zoning issues with the host government before the embassy could be sold. OBO officials told us that the old embassy was zoned for diplomatic use and that the process to change the zoning to mixed-use is under way. OBO and post officials have worked with the host government, and post officials believe the decision to zone the property for commercial and residential use will increase the disposal price of the property.

State Uses Data on Property Disposal Costs in Managing Real Property, but Data May Be Incomplete

OBO collects data on costs associated with unneeded properties identified for disposal to track costs associated with properties before their disposal, but the data do not specify costs associated with individual properties.[17] Once OBO approves a property as unneeded, each post should charge a specific internal accounting code designated for property acquisition and disposal costs.

Source: GAO.| GAO-14-769.

Figure 6. Former Belgrade Embassy.

OBO officials told us that each post is required to charge costs for property to this code so OBO can track the costs to maintain the property before the property is disposed by State. For example, these types of costs would include utilities, legal fees, and security services. Posts charged approximately $11.1 million to this code from fiscal year 2008 through 2013, according to the data provided by OBO.

We found that the four posts we visited did not use this code consistently. State's *Foreign Affairs Handbook* instructs posts to use the code to record costs related to the disposal of unneeded real property, but does not describe in detail the types of costs that can be charged to this account.[18] Specifically, the *Foreign Affairs Handbook* includes the following information on this accounting code: "7541 Real Estate-Program Costs: Costs in support of the acquisition and disposal of State real property." OBO officials told us costs for unneeded properties that should be charged to this code include disposal costs for government-owned buildings, such as guard, maintenance, utility, and other building operating costs of vacant/unneeded property until sold. Although State relies on this account to monitor costs associated with disposal of unneeded properties, on our site visits we found that officials at one post did not know they could use this account for costs related to properties identified for disposal, such as utility bills and condominium fees while marketing the property. This post charged these costs to its routine maintenance account not intended for unneeded properties. Post officials thought the code for unneeded properties was used to process the disposal, and not for ongoing costs related to the property while the property was being marketed for disposal. Officials at the other two posts we visited that had unneeded property for disposal used the code to charge all of their related costs while they marketed the property for disposal.[19] We found posts in other countries with unneeded properties identified for disposal in fiscal year 2013 had not charged expenses to this account during that fiscal year such as posts in Jamaica, Ukraine, Tunisia, and Namibia.

OMB's capital-planning guidance states that reliable data are critical to managing assets effectively.[20] According to this guidance, only valid, complete, relevant, reliable, and timely data can help the agency make informed decisions regarding the allocation of resources. Additionally, government-wide internal control standards state that pertinent financial and operating information should be recorded and communicated to management and others within a time frame that enables them to carry out their internal control and other responsibilities.[21] State will be unable to capture and maintain complete and accurate information on the operating costs for properties identified for disposal if posts do not consistently charge costs related to these properties to the designated account. This raises questions about the extent to which posts worldwide are using the code as State intends and the extent to which State is receiving accurate and comprehensive cost information about its properties. For example, State may not have the information it needs to make a decision to accept or decline an offer for a property when attempting to maximize revenue for a property disposal. In addition, posts may not have sufficient funding for routine property maintenance because they are using their designated routine maintenance funds on unneeded properties, which could reduce the amount of funding they have available for maintenance of other properties. This could impact the upkeep of posts' current real-property portfolio and increase the amount for deferred maintenance. We have previously reported that deferring maintenance and repair can reduce the overall life of federal facilities, lead to higher cost in the long term, and pose risks to safety and agencies' missions.[22]

State Is Attempting to Reduce Its Reliance on Leased Space and Related Costs but Faces Challenges

OBO officials said that they would like to reduce the number of leased properties in State's portfolio and increase federally owned property. OBO officials told us that owning more housing will save on aspects of lease costs, such as exchange-rate fluctuations, rapid inflation, and rising property rents. The officials added that currently 15 percent of State's residential properties are federally owned, but officials would like to eventually increase this number to 40 percent. They told us that based on the average cost of a property's acquisition, along with expected reinvestment of disposal proceeds on a yearly basis; it will take about 50 years to reach this ownership target. Officials believe it is not cost effective or feasible to own 100 percent of properties due to the inability to own properties in some countries, high maintenance costs of owning properties in some countries, and the lack of flexibility in dealing with staffing changes. OBO officials told us that they consider the unique facts and circumstances of each country when deciding whether to lease or acquire properties. We have previously reported on the federal government's over-reliance on leasing, which could be more expensive in the long term than the cost to acquire property.[23]

State relies on its Opportunity Purchase Program to fund real property acquisitions, and to reduce its need to lease space. The Opportunity Purchase Program reinvests proceeds from property disposals to acquire real properties other than new embassy construction. According to OBO officials, the program allows State to acquire properties in order to avoid costs because State officials conduct a lease-versus-purchase analysis to measure savings from owning rather than leasing over an expected time frame they plan to retain a property. OBO officials told us that over the last several years the program has generated investment returns from its acquisitions that typically range from 7 percent to 10 percent. As funding from disposals becomes available, OBO reviews attractive purchasing markets and security needs at the approximately 275 posts and narrows down purchasing opportunities to 12 to 15 posts. OBO officials told us they notify the post that they have been selected for the program, and the post provides acquisition opportunities for OBO to review. OBO officials told us that disposals are unpredictable to forecast on an annual basis, making planning and funding for these acquisitions difficult. The Belgrade post is an example of where State has employed the Opportunity Purchase Program. State acquired four residential units in Belgrade for approximately $2.1 million in fiscal year 2013 (see fig. 7). According to OBO, from fiscal year 2006 through 2013, the Opportunity Purchase Program has produced approximately $16 million annually in lease cost avoidance and will provide another projected $6 million in lease cost avoidance once all pending acquisitions are completed.

Source: GAO.| GAO-14-769.

Figure 7. Residential Property Acquired in Belgrade.

Post and OBO officials we interviewed echoed similar views on the preference of owning versus leasing based on the real estate market in each post's location. Post and OBO officials told us that the conditions of a specific location, such as the local real estate market and the mission of the post influence the decision to own or lease. For example, post officials in Helsinki told us that properties are costly to acquire and expensive to maintain in the area. They said leasing is a better option because it provides flexibility when staffing changes occur, and the property owners in the area are reliable and responsive. Post officials in Sarajevo told us that because of the instability of the real estate market and possible future changes in embassy staffing, it is more practical to lease residential housing. On the other hand, post officials in Belgrade told us that they would like to own more residential units because of the difficulty in finding quality housing to lease. OBO officials told us they prefer a mix of owned and leased housing to provide a stable housing pool, manage rental costs, and provide flexibility as mission requirements change, and officials seek to acquire housing in markets where they can acquire quality housing and where it is cost effective to own rather than lease.

In addition to acquisitions, OBO and post officials described several steps they have taken to reduce costs associated with leasing:

- OBO reviews its highest cost expiring leases annually to determine if State is obtaining a market rate for these properties and if leases should be renewed or replaced. Officials told us that this review includes 100 of the most costly leases worldwide and is used to assist posts that take the lead in monitoring and securing lease renewals.

OBO officials told us that in fiscal year 2014 after this review, they determined that 30 percent of leases were prospects for exploring whether rents can be reduced. Under FAM, appraisals or other documentation such as a market study or a design review for the acquisition and renewal of major leases are used for each transaction.24 OBO meets this guidance by providing fair-market rental estimates, market studies, surveys, and legal direction for posts.

- OBO is attempting to maximize the cost effectiveness of its leased portfolio. OBO officials told us they implemented a rental benchmark program in 2007 to help ensure the U.S. government pays the prevailing market rate, and does not overpay for leased housing. Officials told us that 25 posts were involved with the program when it began in 2007 and that it covered 171 posts in 2013.25 OBO works with posts and contracts with real estate experts to provide rental ceilings for leased residential properties at each post. OBO uses these ceilings to set a cap on the amount a post can spend on leased residential property, and if a post exceeds that cap, OBO must approve a waiver.26 OBO officials told us that they conduct a quarterly review of the posts to see that they are in compliance and that the program incentivizes posts to stay within their rental ceilings to secure cost-effective leases. Belgrade post officials spoke highly of the program as it has reduced the post's administrative burden in seeking waivers, by providing a more realistic ceiling, which has allowed the post to secure housing in a timelier manner. Also, OBO officials told us that the program has resulted in savings by slowing down the growth of leasing costs.
- Post and OBO officials told us that they proactively renegotiate leases to reduce costs. Officials at all four posts we visited told us that their locally employed staff had established strong working relationships with property owners from years of real estate experience. Post officials told us that the locally employed staff were instrumental in negotiating reduced lease costs. For example, one post official told us that the post secured office space for 30 percent below market value, and officials from another post told us that they were in the process of securing a new leased warehouse space that would save $50,000 to $80,000 per year due to the expertise of the local staff working at the post. In addition, posts and OBO have successfully renegotiated leases since fiscal year 2011 in St. Petersburg, Russia; Paris, France; La Paz, Bolivia; Budapest, Hungary; and Tokyo, Japan that have produced

approximately $3.5 million in savings. Also, OBO officials told us that in their estimation, the lease waiver program avoided $43 million in lease costs by working with overseas posts to locate less costly property, renegotiating lease terms, and by rejecting approval of proposed rent increases or higher cost replacement properties.

State Was Unable to Provide All Documentation on Real Property Transactions

OBO could not provide us all the real property files we requested for acquisitions and disposals between fiscal year 2008 through 2013, except for the files pertaining to leases. Specifically, we requested 202 files which included property disposals, acquisitions, and leases, but OBO stated it was only able to provide 90 of the files because these files were not centrally located and too time consuming to find and provide within the timeframe of our review. OBO agreed to provide us "core" documents for acquisition and disposal files; however some of the documentation was missing in the files we reviewed. In addition, although OBO was able to provide all the lease files requested we found the lease files to be incomplete based on *FAM* and OMB guidance (see Table 3). Without the missing files and documentation, it is unclear how efficiently and effectively State is managing its overseas real property.

Table 3. Department of State Overseas Real Property Files Requested and Provided Fiscal Years 2008 to 2013

File type	Number of files requested	Number of files provided
Acquisitions	72	34
Disposals	94	20
Leases	36	36

Source: GAO analysis of Department of State information. | GAO-14-769.

Acquisitions and Disposals: Under *FAM,* OBO and posts should create and preserve records containing adequate and proper documentation of the decisions, procedures, and transactions or operations of the Department and posts.[27] Further, *Standards for Internal Control* in the federal government states that an agency should establish control activities to ensure that the agency completely and accurately records all transactions.[28] These standards explain that control activities include activities such as the creation and maintenance of related records that provide evidence of execution of these activities as well as appropriate documentation. OBO told us that they were unable to provide all of the information for acquisitions and disposals as requested because files were not centrally located, maintained by different groups within State, and too time consuming to find and provide within the time frame of our review.[29] Thus, OBO officials agreed to provide what they considered "core" documents, which were a subset of the documentation we requested based on our analysis of *FAM* and OMB guidance.[30] State was able to provide most of the "core" documents agreed to, although some of the documentation was missing. For example, we found instances of acquisition files missing deeds and disposal files missing deposit slips, which were both core documents State agreed to provide. Furthermore, since we received only core documents, we could not determine whether the work to meet additional FAM and OMB guidance was conducted and the records were missing, or if this work was not conducted at all. Without this information, it is unclear whether State is consistently following its internal *FAM* and external OMB guidance, and how State officials made real property decisions. These findings are similar to those of State's IG which found significant vulnerabilities due to inadequate file documentation that could potentially expose the Department to substantial financial losses.[31]

Leases: State was able to provide all 36 of the requested lease files, but some documentation listed in *FAM* and OMB guidance was not in 30 of the 36 of the files we reviewed. For example, State guidance directs OBO to complete documentation for leases such as: a lease agreement and documentation of OBO's approval. Additionally, OMB directs executive branch agencies, such as State, to conduct a lease-versus-purchase analysis when deciding to lease or acquire properties to ensure all leases are justified as preferable to direct U.S. government purchase and ownership.[32] All 36 files contained a lease agreement. However, only 6 of the 36 files contained all of the information that *FAM* directs State to retain and that State agreed to provide. These findings are similar to those of State's IG which found that the Department's process to monitor lease information provided by posts was not always effective. The IG found numerous recorded lease terms that did not agree with supporting documentation.[33] We found that 30 of 36 files lacked either documentation of OBO's approval or a lease-versus-purchase analysis, or both. OBO officials told us they do not conduct a lease versus purchase analysis when purchasing is not an option, such as in cases where there is a lack of sufficient funding or the property is in a country that does not allow non-domestic ownership. According to OBO, 6 of the 36 leases in our review were for space in a country that did not allow non-domestic ownership; however, the files did not include documentation that this was the case. We have previously found that without a lease-versuspurchase analysis, decision makers lack financial information on the longterm decisions to lease rather than own. Also, we have previously found that when this analysis has been conducted in the federal government that such analysis has identified savings from owning versus leasing.[34]

CONCLUSION

State manages a multibillion dollar portfolio of buildings, land, and structures at approximately 275 posts throughout the world and has $7.5 billion in projects currently under design and construction. The Department has taken a number of measures to improve management of these properties. These measures include actively identifying unneeded properties, providing posts with rental cost parameters, and other cost-saving initiatives. Despite these steps in managing the real property portfolio, State cannot identify the cost associated with properties identified for disposal, which may compromise State's ability to make fully informed decisions because of unclear guidance. Furthermore, State could not provide some key documents we requested for our review pertaining to acquisitions, disposals, and leases of its properties worldwide. As a result, the Department may not be able to ensure that it is making cost-effective decisions about properties. Improvements in these areas will become more important as State constructs additional NECs and disposes properties no longer needed when personnel relocate to new facilities.

RECOMMENDATIONS FOR EXECUTIVE ACTION

To improve State's management of real property overseas and enhance State's accountability and ability to track real-property management decisions, the Secretary of State should take the following four actions:

1. Clarify accounting-code guidance to the posts for tracking expenses related to disposal of unneeded properties.

2. Take steps to ensure that documents related to real property acquisitions are prepared and retained in accordance with *FAM* and OMB guidance.
3. Take steps to ensure that documents related to real property disposals are prepared and retained in accordance with *FAM* and OMB guidance.
4. Take steps to ensure that documents related to real property leases are prepared and retained in accordance with *FAM* and OMB guidance.

AGENCY COMMENTS

We provided a draft of this product to the Department of State (State) for review and comment. In written comments, State concurred with the report's recommendations. State provided technical clarifications that were incorporated as appropriate.

David J. Wise
Director
Physical Infrastructure Issues

Michael J. Courts
Director
International Affairs and Trade

APPENDIX I: SCOPE AND METHODOLOGY

To determine what is known about the Department of State's (State) real property inventory, we reviewed State's Federal Real Property Profile (FRPP) data for fiscal years 2008 through 2013—the time period of our review. Additionally, we reviewed State's real property reports to Congress and compared these with State's annual FRPP reports to the General Services Administration. We determined that FRPP data were sufficiently reliable for the purpose of reporting approximate numbers of properties in State's portfolio by interviewing knowledgeable Bureau of Overseas Buildings Operations (OBO) and post officials about data quality assurance procedures and reviewing related documentation, including previous GAO and State Inspector

General (IG) reports, data dictionaries and user manuals, and data verification practices. We also reviewed State's internal report on costs associated with properties identified for disposal to determine costs for unneeded properties that State is selling. To evaluate the reliability of State's real property database we interviewed OBO and post officials and locally employed staff responsible for entering real property data at the four posts we visited. We also examined OBO's policies and processes for entering information into its real property database and issues affecting quality control over this information. Although we identified data reliability issues for some facilities in State's real property database, as those issues generally involved the classification or description of facilities, we determined that the data were sufficiently reliable to describe the approximate number of U.S. properties overseas.[1]

To determine what factors State considers in managing its real property portfolio and the extent to which it documents its decision-making process, we reviewed sections of the *Foreign Affairs Manual* (*FAM*) applicable to property management overseas and documents prepared by State officials in response to our questions. We reviewed State's data on costs associated with unneeded properties identified for disposal for fiscal years 2008 through 2013. We found the data had limitations, which we discuss in the report. We reviewed documentation that State provided for its real property disposals, acquisitions, and leases from fiscal years 2008 through 2013. We requested files on all 94 property disposals and 72 property acquisitions reported during this period. State provided 20 of the 94 disposal files we requested and 34 of the 72 acquisition files, which included all of the 2013 files.[2] We also requested, and were provided with, all 36 major leases with $500,000 or more in annual rent, as defined in the *FAM*, that were active from fiscal years 2008 through 2013 and still were listed as active in FRPP at the end of fiscal year 2013. To evaluate the completeness of these files we compared State's documentation of real property disposals, acquisitions, and leases to the documentation directives listed in *FAM* and relevant Office of Management and Budget (OMB) Circulars. We also obtained information on how State reinvested revenue generated from property disposals between fiscal years 2008 through 2013. While our review of these disposals, acquisitions, and leases provides key insights and illustrates recent products of State's real property policies and guidance, the results of our review should not be used to make generalizations about all State disposals, acquisitions, and leases.

We interviewed State Department officials at OBO and at four selected posts (Belgrade, Serbia; Helsinki, Finland; London, United Kingdom; and Sarajevo, Bosnia, and Herzegovina) to gather information on unneeded properties, disposals, acquisitions, and leases. We selected these posts because they had (1) ongoing or recently completed embassy construction or renovation projects without disposing of properties, (2) properties reported as identified for disposal for multiple years without being disposed of, and (3) a mix of owned and leased properties. We based our site visit selection on these factors in order to observe posts with (1) higher numbers of property disposals than other posts due to recently completed or ongoing construction of new embassies, (2) persistent challenges in selling unneeded properties, and (3) experience managing both owned and leased properties. The results of the case studies provide insight into State's management and decision-making practices but cannot be generalized for the purposes of this review.

We conducted this performance audit from June 2013 to September 2014 in accordance with generally accepted government auditing standards. Those standards require that we plan and perform the audit to obtain sufficient, appropriate evidence to provide a reasonable basis for our findings and conclusions based on our audit objectives. We believe that the evidence obtained provides a reasonable basis for our findings and conclusions based on our audit objectives.

End Notes

[1] GAO, State Department: Sale of Unneeded Overseas Property Has Increased, but Further Improvements are Necessary, GAO-02-590 (Washington D.C.: June 11, 2002), and Overseas Real Estate: Millions of Dollars Could Be Generated by Selling Unneeded Real Estate, GAO/NSIAD-96-36 (Washington D.C.: Apr. 23, 1996).

[2] For the purposes of this report, we use the term "unneeded" property to encompass the terms "excess, underutilized, surplus, and obsolete" property. In our 2002 report (GAO-02-590), we recommended that the Secretary of State take action to improve the accuracy of the real property inventory in order to improve State's ability to identify properties that may be available for disposal.

[3] GAO, High-Risk Series An Update, GAO-13-283 (Washington D.C.: February 2013).

[4] An acquisition or disposal reported to Congress may include multiple properties. For example, State, in fiscal year 2010, acquired a housing compound of 60 units in Nairobi that was reported to Congress as one property acquisition.

[5] U.S. Department of State, Foreign Affairs Manual: Leased Space Abroad, 15 FAM 311 (Apr. 21, 2014). Under the FAM, annual rent is one of several ways a lease can be categorized as a major lease.

[6] 22 U.S.C. §§ 291-303. For the purposes of this report, we identify real property purchases as acquisitions, and we identify current leases and lease acquisitions as leases.

[7] Federal Real Property Asset Management, Executive. Order No. 13327, 69 Fed. Reg. 5897 (Feb. 6, 2004).

[8] Pub. L. No. 106-113, Div. B, tit. VI (1999). State elaborates on these requirements in the U.S. Department of State Foreign Affairs Handbook, 12 FAH-5.

[9] Consolidated Appropriations Act, 2005, Pub. L. No. 108-447, Div. B, tit.VI, § 629 (2004).

[10] According to OBO officials, reasons for leasing a large percentage of State's property include a large increase in overseas staffing, which translates directly into more leased housing; host country restrictions on owning properties; limited funding for purchasing properties; and the need for flexibility to respond to staffing changes at posts.

[11] As directed by the conference report accompanying the Consolidated Appropriations Act, 1997, State reports its real property acquisitions and sales to Congress quarterly. H.R. Conf. Rep. No. 104-863 (1996). We used these reports to determine acquisitions and sales between fiscal year 2008 to 2013.

[12] 22 U.S.C. § 303.

[13] United States Department of State, Office of Inspector General, and Report of Inspection: Embassy Brasilia and Constituent Posts, Brazil, ISP-I-08-15A (Washington D.C.: March 2008).

[14] The Sarajevo post does not own any property other than its embassy compound so the guidance for identifying unneeded property does not directly apply to it.

[15] These proceeds were reinvested within the same post by special arrangement. The Consolidated Appropriations Act, 2012 provided a limitation on the use of funds, other than funds from real property sales located in London, for the site acquisition and mitigation, planning, design, or construction of the new London embassy. Pub. L. No. 112- 74, Div. I, tit. VII, § 7004(f)(1), 125 Stat. 786, 1194 (2011). The Consolidated Appropriations Act, 2014 stated that this limitation would remain in effect during fiscal year 2014. Pub. L. No. 113-76. Div. K, tit. VII, § 7004(e)(1), 128 Stat. 5, 492 (2014).

[16] Since the time of our visit, OBO officials told us that the firm marketing the Belgrade embassy was terminated, and they are in the process of selecting a new firm.

[17] GAO has found that agencies have difficulty in reporting annual operating costs at the building level. GAO, Federal Real Property: National Strategy and Better Data Needed to Improve Management of Excess and Underutilized Property GAO-12-645 (Washington D.C.: June 20, 2012).

[18] U.S. Department of State, Foreign Affairs Handbook, 4 FAH-1 H-510 and 4 FAH-1 H520, 120.

[19] Three of the four posts we visited had properties for disposal. Sarajevo did not have any properties for disposal.

[20] Office of Management and Budget, Management's Responsibility for Internal Controls, OMB Circular A-123, (Washington D.C.: September 21, 2004).

[21] GAO, Standards for Internal Control in the Federal Government, GAO/AIMD-00-21.3.1 (Washington D.C.: November 1, 1999).

[22] GAO, Federal Real Property: Improved Transparency Could Help Efforts to Manage Agencies' Repair and Maintenance Backlogs, GAO-14-188 (Washington D.C.: January 23, 2014).

[23] GAO, Federal Real Property: Greater Transparency and Strategic Focus Needed for High-Value GSA Leases, GAO-13-744 (Washington D.C.: Sept. 19, 2013).

[24] 15 FAM 312.

[25] OBO requires all posts, with the exception of posts with fewer than 10 short-term leased residential properties, unaccompanied posts, and posts without an established rental housing market to participate in the rental benchmark program. It is anticipated that 180 posts will come into the rental benchmark program.

[26] According to FAM guidance, lease waivers are required for (1) all leased property that exceeds approved rental benchmarks, (2) all housing assignments that exceed the maximum space standards, (3) all residential leases that have an annual rent in excess of $50,000, (4) non-residential leases, and (5) leases for all designated residences regardless of cost. 15 FAM 321.

[27] U.S. Department of State, Foreign Affairs Manual: Real Property Acquisition Abroad, 15 FAM 400 (Oct. 31, 2013).

[28] GAO/AIMD-00-21-3-1.

[29] We requested the entire file based on analysis of FAM and OMB guidance. State could not provide us with the following requested documentation for all acquisitions and disposals: Acquisitions: (1) need to obtain two independent appraisals and (2) lease versus purchase analysis. Disposals: (1) two independent appraisals, (2) evidence of use of a real estate broker, and (3) evidence on the use of a local legal counsel.

[30] OBO agreed to provide us four types of "core" acquisition documents including: (1) cables authorizing closing, (2) action memo authorizing closing, (3) deed, and (4) a voucher documenting a transfer of funds. OBO agreed to provide five types of "core" disposal documents including: (1) reconciled estimate of value memo, (2) action memo authorizing closing, (3) sales agreement contract, (4) general receipt, and (5) deposit slip.

[31] United States Department of State and Broadcasting Board of Governors, Office of Inspector General, Management Alert (Contract File Deficiencies), MAA-0002, (Washington D.C.: Mar. 20, 2014).

[32] Office of Management and Budget, Guidelines and Discount Rates for Benefit-Cost Analysis of Federal Programs, OMB Circular No. A-94 Revised (Oct. 29, 1992).

[33] Kearney and Company, Independent Auditors Report, AUD-FM-14-10, (Alexandria, VA: Dec. 12, 2013).

[34] GAO-13-744.

End Notes for Appendix I

[1] See GAO, Diplomatic Security: Overseas Facilities May Face Greater Risks Due to Gaps in Security-Related Activities, Standards, and Policies, GAO-14-655 (Washington D.C.: June 25, 2014).

[2] An acquisition or disposal reported to Congress may include multiple properties. For example, State, in fiscal year 2010, acquired a housing compound of 60 units in Nairobi that was reported to Congress as one property acquisition.

In: Federal Real Property: Analyses of Key Issues ISBN: 978-1-63482-278-7
Editor: Adam B. Clark

Chapter 4

OVERVIEW OF FEDERAL REAL PROPERTY DISPOSAL REQUIREMENTS AND PROCEDURES*

Garrett Hatch, Daniel H. Else, Linda Luther, David M. Bearden and Kristina Alexander

SUMMARY

The federal government holds thousands of properties that agencies no longer need to accomplish their missions. When the government disposes of unneeded properties—through transfer, donation, or sale—it generates savings by eliminating maintenance costs. In addition, when state or local governments, nonprofits, or businesses acquire unneeded federal properties, they may be used to provide services to the public, such as temporary housing, or contribute to economic development.

The General Services Administration (GSA) plays a central role in disposing of unneeded property at most federal agencies. The Federal Real Property and Administrative Services Act of 1949 (Property Act) gives GSA the authority to dispose of real property at all federal agencies unless they have independent statutory authority to dispose of their own properties themselves. A number of agencies have independent disposal authority—ranging from limited to broad in scope—including two of the

* This is an edited, reformatted and augmented version of a Congressional Research Service publication R43818, prepared for Members and Committees of Congress dated December 10, 2014.

largest federal landholders, the U.S. Postal Service (USPS) and the Department of Defense.

When an agency notifies GSA that it has unneeded real property, GSA first offers to transfer the property to another federal agency, which must pay fair market value for it. If no other agency wishes to acquire the property, GSA may then convey it to a state or local government, or a qualified nonprofit, for up to a 100% discount—provided it is used for an approved public benefit. Should a state or local government or qualified nonprofit wish to acquire the property for a use other than one of the approved public benefits, GSA has the option to sell the property to them at fair market value. Finally, if the property is not sold to a public or nonprofit entity, it is offered for sale to the public.

The disposal of a federal property may be subject to a number of environmental requirements and historic preservation mandates, although which requirements apply depends on a number of site-specific conditions. Three principal federal statutes govern the environmental review process, identification and remediation of hazardous substances, and historic preservation: the National Environmental Protection Act (NEPA), the Comprehensive Environmental Response, Compensation and Liability Act of 1980 (CERCLA), and the National Historic Preservation Act (NHPA).

Among the agencies with independent statutory disposal authority, USPS has the greatest autonomy. The Postal Service has, in essence, been granted the authority to dispose of its properties as it deems appropriate, without the assistance of GSA. DOD also has independent statutory disposal authority, but of a more limited scope. DOD must use GSA to dispose of all properties that do not otherwise fall under the scope of special, temporary disposal authorities, commonly referred to as Base Realignment and Closure (BRAC) legislation.

INTRODUCTION

Federal executive branch agencies hold an extensive real property portfolio that includes more than 871,000 buildings and structures, and 40 million acres of land worldwide.[1] These assets have been acquired over a period of decades to help agencies fulfill their diverse missions. Agencies hold properties with a range of uses, including barracks, health clinics, warehouses, laboratories, national parks, boat docks, and offices. As agencies' missions change over time, so, too, do their real property needs, thereby rendering some assets less useful or unneeded altogether. Healthcare provided by the Department of Veterans Affairs (VA), for example, has shifted in recent decades from predominately hospital-based inpatient care to a greater reliance on clinics and outpatient care, with a resulting change in space needs.[2] Similarly, the Department of Defense (DOD) reduced its force structure by 36% after the Cold War ended, and has engaged in several rounds of base realignments and installation closures.[3]

Real property disposition is the process by which federal agencies identify and then transfer, donate, or sell facilities and land they no longer need. Disposition is an important asset-management function because the costs of maintaining unneeded properties can be substantial. In FY2013, for example, the government disposed of 21,464 unneeded properties with annual operating costs of $411 million.[4] Savings generated by the disposal of unneeded properties might be applied to pressing real property needs, such as improving building security or repairing existing facilities, or towards other pressing policy issues, such as reducing the national debt. Disposition is also important because it is a mechanism by which state and local governments, nonprofit organizations, and businesses may acquire federal property. In the hands of nonfederal entities, the previously underutilized properties may be used to provide services to the public, such as temporary housing, or contribute to economic development.

This report begins with an explanation of the central role played by the General Services Administration (GSA) in the disposal of federal real property at most agencies. It then provides a discussion of the unique disposal processes at DOD and the U.S. Postal Service (USPS), which each have independent statutory authority to dispose of their own properties. It concludes with an overview of the environmental and historic preservation requirements that apply to the disposal of properties at all federal agencies.

Centralized Disposal Through the General Services Administration[5]

The Federal Real Property and Administrative Services Act of 1949 (Property Act) applies to real property held by most federal agencies.[6] The Property Act gives GSA the authority to dispose of real property that federal agencies no longer need, although some agencies have been granted the authority to dispose of some or all of their own property.[7] Under the provisions of the Property Act, GSA disposes of federal real property for federal agencies that lack independent statutory authority to do so themselves. Agencies without independent disposal authority generally follow the process described in this section. The disposal processes at two landholding agencies with broad independent disposal authority, DOD and USPS, are also discussed in this report.

Federal Transfer

In order to identify properties that agencies no longer need, each agency is required to conduct an annual survey of its real property holdings. Properties that are no longer needed are reported to GSA as "excess."[8] GSA then physically inspects each excess property and hires a licensed appraiser to evaluate its fair market value.[9] Next, GSA sends a written Notice of Availability describing the property to other federal agencies and posts information about the property on its Property Disposal Resource Center website.[10] Agencies may also identify unneeded assets available for transfer through the Federal Real Property Profile (FRPP), a database of the buildings, structures, and land held by federal agencies.[11] If an agency wants to acquire an excess property, it must respond to the Notice of Availability within 30 days and then submit a formal request for the property to be transferred within 60 days from the date the notice expires. Agencies are required to pay fair market value to acquire excess property, although there are a number of circumstances under which an exception to this requirement may be approved.[12]

Public Benefit Conveyance

If no federal agency wants an unneeded property, it is declared "surplus" and made available to state and local governments, and nonprofits.[13] These entities may have surplus property transferred to them for a discount of up to 100% of fair market value, provided they use the property for a public benefit.[14] This type of transfer is called a public benefit conveyance, and to qualify, the property must be used for one of the following purposes:

- Homeless services
- Corrections
- Law enforcement
- Public health

- Drug rehabilitation
- Education
- Parks and recreation
- Seaport facilities
- Wildlife conservation
- Highways
- Emergency Management Response
- Historic monuments
- Public airports
- Housing

Each public benefit category has a federal agency, called a sponsor, that oversees conveyances for that purpose. Generally, sponsoring agencies have expertise in the policy areas they sponsor. The Federal Aviation Administration, for example, is the sponsoring agency for public airport conveyances.[15]

Pursuant to Title V of the McKinney-Vento Homeless Assistance Act, surplus properties must be made available for serving the homeless before being made available for other public benefit uses.[16] The Department of Housing and Urban Development (HUD) is responsible for reviewing surplus property to determine if it is suitable for homeless use. If a property is determined to be unsuitable for homeless use, then it becomes available for other public uses at that time. If HUD determines a surplus property is suitable, however, it publishes a notice to that effect in the *Federal Register*. State and local governments, and nonprofits, are given 60 days to notify the sponsoring agency, the Department of Health and Human Services (HHS), that they are interested in using the property for serving the homeless.[17] If HHS receives an expression of interest within the 60-day window, the property may not be made available for any other purpose until action on the request is complete. If no interest is expressed, then the property becomes available for other public benefit uses.[18] GSA advertises its availability by contacting state and local officials and known nonprofits with an interest in the property. GSA may also post notices in city halls, state capitols, and other appropriate locations.[19] The sponsoring agency is generally responsible for distributing, reviewing, and approving applications; conveying the property to the recipient; and monitoring the use of the property after it has been transferred, although GSA assists some agencies with these duties.[20] If the recipient of a conveyed property fails to use the property as agreed—by building a retail center on property conveyed for a public park, for example—then the property may revert back to the federal government.

Negotiated Sale

Surplus property that is not disposed of through the public benefit conveyance process may be sold to state and local governments at fair market value.[21] In essence, state and local governments are given the right of first refusal—they are allowed an opportunity to purchase surplus property before the property is offered for sale to the general public. Federal real property regulations permit negotiated sales when "a public benefit, which would not be realized from a competitive sale, will result from the negotiated sale."[22] The regulations do not specify what types of activities would qualify, but GSA guidance notes that a state or local government can use property "according to its own redevelopment needs," including economic development.[23]

Public Sale

Surplus properties that are still available after screening for public benefit conveyance and negotiated sale may be offered for public sale. The property is advertised in local newspapers, regional or national publications, and the U.S. Real Estate Sales list, and may also be found on GSA's website.[24] The appraised value of a property is used as a guideline for initial pricing, and properties are sold through sealed bids, physical auctions, and Internet auctions.[25]

Real Property Disposal at USPS and DOD

DOD and USPS are two of the three largest federal landholding agencies, as measured by owned square feet. DOD is the largest, with more than 1.7 billion square feet of owned space in its inventory, while USPS is the third largest with 197 million square feet of owned space.[26] Both DOD and USPS have independent statutory authority to dispose of unneeded real property, although the scope of that authority differs. While USPS has been given autonomy in disposing of all of its properties, DOD's disposal authorities are more limited and more complicated. The remainder of this section discusses the disposal process at each agency.

U.S. Postal Service[27]

Congress has given USPS independent statutory authority to dispose of its real estate as it deems proper.[28] USPS may

> acquire, in any lawful manner, such personal or real property, or any interest therein, as it deems necessary or convenient in the transaction of its business; to hold, maintain, sell, lease, or otherwise dispose of such property or any interest therein; and to provide services in connection therewith and charges therefor.[29]

Allowing USPS to make decisions over its real estate and property holdings has been viewed as integral to the concept of the USPS as encapsulated in the Postal Reorganization Act (PRA).[30] This 1970 statute replaced the Post Office Department (an appropriations-dependent agency) with the U.S. Postal Service (a financially self-supporting "independent establishment of the executive branch."[31] The PRA assigned USPS the "general duty" to "maintain an efficient system of collection, sorting, and delivery of the mail nationwide."[32] In order to carry out this obligation, Congress provided USPS with a number of powers to generate revenue and control its operational costs, including the authority to "determine the need for post offices, postal and training facilities and equipment, and ... provide such offices, facilities, and equipment as it determines are needed."[33] This authority over real property has helped USPS respond to shifts in population by expanding its presence in areas where the number of people and businesses was growing, and scaling back USPS's operational footprint in places where population was decreasing. This authority over its property and facilities also permits USPS to alter its logistical (mail-moving) network to accommodate mail volume changes and technological developments in mail processing.[34]

Disposal of Postal Properties

USPS policy is to dispose of excess real property under the terms and conditions that provide the greatest value to the Postal Service. Disposition may be by sale, exchange, outlease, sublease, or by other means determined to be in the best interest of the Postal Service.[35] In addition, USPS has employed private real estate companies to sell some of its excess or unneeded properties.[36] The agency also has auctioned some of its properties, including the Chicago Main Post Office, a 14- story property of 3 million square feet.[37]

Both federal law and the USPS's rules prescribe a post office closure process, which takes at least 120 days.[38] The USPS must notify members of the public who may be affected by the closure, and hold a 60-day comment period prior to closing a post office. Should the USPS decide to close a post office, the public has 30 days to appeal the decision to the Postal Regulatory Commission (PRC).[39] Sixty days after USPS has made a closure decision, the agency may shut down a post office, regardless of the outcome of the PRC's review.[40] Federal statute does not require USPS to take public comment when it disposes of properties that are not post offices, such as properties utilized as office space.

Department of Defense[41]

DOD comprises the Office of the Secretary of Defense (which includes all defense agencies and field activities); the Joint Chiefs of Staff; the Combatant Commands (such as Central Command, Northern Command, and Strategic Command); and the military departments of the Army, Navy, and Air Force. All real property is placed under the jurisdiction of one of the military departments.

Individual defense facilities fall under the immediate responsibility of a local installation military officer who could be referred to as the garrison commander, the base wing commander, the base commander, or the station commander, depending on the service administering the site.

The following sections will first describe the identification and disposal of military real property under routine practice, then the special procedures that were authorized under the Defense Base Closure and Realignment Act of 1990,[42] as amended. The latter process is commonly known as a Base Realignment and Closure (BRAC) round.

Routine Disposal of Real Property

The officers entrusted with administration of a defense site are required to periodically review the current and anticipated utilization of its land and facilities. A change in military strategy or doctrine, mission, operations, military equipment, or units based at a given facility could similarly change the need for site infrastructure. If the officer in charge determines that certain real property is no longer needed, he or she forwards a recommendation to "excess" the property up the appropriate chain of command. The final authority for declaring real property to be excess rests with the Secretary of the relevant military department, though the responsibility for managing real property inventory is usually delegated to an Assistant Secretary.

Once defense property is identified as excess, the administering military service submits a report to GSA. Other defense organizations, both active and reserve, may request that all or part of it be transferred to them. GSA then screens the property for potential use by other federal agencies. If no agency expresses interest within a reasonable period, the property is considered surplus, and GSA then directs and supervises the disposal process discussed elsewhere in this report.

Congress has imposed several statutory disposal restrictions and reporting requirements on DOD and codified them in a number of sections within Title 10 (Armed Forces) of the United States Code. Included among them are

- 10 U.S.C. 2662, which requires that, for real property with an estimated value in excess of $750,000, the Secretary concerned report to the House and Senate Committees on Armed Services any (1) transfer of real property to another federal agency or another military department or to a State, or (2) report of excess real property to a disposal agency (such as GSA), wait 30 days (14 days if the report is made by electronic medium) before undertaking the transaction, and report again within 30 days of entering into the transaction;
- 10 U.S.C. 2694a, a section that authorizes a Secretary to convey to a State, one of its political subdivisions, or a nonprofit organization any surplus real property under his jurisdiction that is suitable for conservation purposes, has been made available for a public benefit conveyance,[43] and is not subject to a pending request for transfer to another federal agency, after notification of the relevant congressional committees and waiting 21 days;
- 10 U.S.C. 2696, which both allows military department secretaries to transfer real property under their jurisdiction between themselves without compensation and requires the GSA Administrator to screen all defense real property for further federal use before a Secretary conveys it under any provision of law enacted after December 31, 1997, though there are some exceptions and special provisions for land intended for use as a correctional facility.

BRAC: Special Temporary Disposal Authorities and Procedures

The cessation of operations and closing of a major military installation will often entail a significant impact on the economy and social structure of the communities in its vicinity. Therefore, successive Secretaries of Defense have found over the past several decades that a number of statutory and political constraints have rendered the process, and prospects, of significantly reducing the defense real property "footprint" problematic.

Since the waning days of the Cold War, Congress has from time to time granted special temporary authority to the Secretary of Defense to carry out wholesale reviews of domestic defense real property with the intention of evaluating and reducing the inventory deemed excess to defense needs and surplus to federal requirements. All told, five defense real property disposal series have thus far been authorized. Though created under different laws, each series has become commonly referred to as a Base Realignment and Closure, or BRAC, round.[44] The most recent authorization for a BRAC round expired on April 15, 2006, so any new effort would have to be authorized by the enactment of a new provision of law.

While BRAC rounds have not seen an alteration of the general three-step process (identification, screening, and disposal), the temporary statutes creating them have added a number of features that enhanced oversight of DOD, offered assistance to the communities affected, and increased the transparency of the mechanism by which garrisons are reconfigured and installations are realigned to new missions or shuttered. In addition, many of the provisions of the McKinneyVento Homeless Assistance Act (42 U.S.C. 11301 et seq.) and the National Environmental Policy Act (42 U.S.C. § 4321 et seq.) have been applied to property closed under BRAC much as they do to other federal surplus property.

The differences between the normal real property disposal process carried out by GSA and that initiated by DOD during a BRAC round can be summarized around their three general phases, identification, screening, and disposal. The details following pertain to the processes used during the most recent (2005) BRAC round carried out under the FY2002 reauthorization of the Defense Base Closure and Realignment Act of 1990.

Identification of Property under BRAC

During the 2005 BRAC round, the Secretary of Defense was required to draw up and submit to Congress a "force-structure plan," based on an assessment by the Secretary of the probable threats to the national security during the 20-year period beginning with FY2005, the probable end-strength levels and major military force units (including land force divisions, carrier and other major combatant vessels, air wings, and other comparable units) needed to meet these threats, and the anticipated levels of funding that will be available for national defense purposes during such period[45] and a comprehensive world-wide inventory of military installations for each military department, with specifications of the number and type of facilities in the active and reserve forces of each military department.[46]

DOD was required in the statute to use a set of eight "final selection criteria," divided into "military value criteria" and "other criteria," in making recommendations for closure or realignment. Roughly paraphrased, the four military value criteria for each installation centered on (1) mission capabilities and readiness, (2) availability of facilities, (3) capacity to absorb mobilization surges, and (4) the cost of operations. Other criteria included (1) timing of potential savings, (2) economic impact on surrounding communities, (3) ability of communities to support the installation, and (4) environmental impact. The statute required that only these criteria be used and that priority consideration be given to the military value criteria.[47]

Once identified by DOD, the Secretary of Defense submitted his list of recommended closures or realignments to an independent nine-member commission for further consideration. Appointed by the President, with congressional input, and confirmed by the Senate, the commission and its staff were required to hold public hearings on the Secretary's recommendations. During its deliberations, the statute allowed the commission to add a new installation to the closure or realignment lists or increase the extent of a realignment only if it determined "that the Secretary deviated substantially from the force-structure plan and final criteria" specified earlier and concluded that its amendment was consistent with both. The statute required the commission to submit its own report to the President by a date certain.

Approval and Implementation of Closures and Realignments

After receiving the commission's report, the President was given a finite period of time to submit to Congress and the commission his approval or disapproval of the commission's recommendations. If he disapproved, in whole or in part, the commission's list of recommendations, he was instructed to state his reasons for doing so. The commission then had approximately one month in which to revise and resubmit its list. A second disapproval would have halted the process.[48]

Once having received the President's certification of approval, Congress gave itself a period of 45 days during which it could pass a joint resolution of disapproval using an expedited procedure laid out in the governing statute. If enacted, such a joint resolution would prevent the Secretary of Defense from carrying out any recommended closure or realignment.[49] If not thereby halted, the statute required the Secretary of Defense to initiate all closures and realignments within two years and complete them within six years of the date that the President recorded his approval.

Disposal of Real Property

The statute provided the Secretary of Defense with authority to offer economic adjustment assistance to any community near a closing or realigning military installation and community planning assistance to communities whose local installations absorb functions during the process.[50] This assistance has usually been channeled through "local redevelopment authorities" (LRA) nominated by the affected communities and so designated by the Secretary of Defense. It is to these LRAs that title to surplus property is usually conveyed.

The base closure acts have also provided other special authorities. Their provisions have directed the GSA Administrator to delegate to the Secretary of Defense his or her authorities to utilize excess properties and dispose of surplus properties for installations being closed or realigned. In addition to being able to dispose of surplus property at below market value through public benefit conveyances, the Secretary has been able to do the same if the LRA has agreed to apply proceeds from the sale or lease of property to the economic redevelopment of the site.

While DOD retains responsibility for the remediation of environmental contamination at former defense sites, the statute places no time limit on either remediation or on the conveyance of the property from the federal government.

ENVIRONMENTAL REQUIREMENTS AND HISTORIC PRESERVATION

The transfer of surplus federal property may be subject to an array of environmental requirements intended to protect human health and safety, natural resources, and cultural resources.[51] Which requirements may apply to the transfer of a property would depend upon the site-specific conditions, such as the presence of wastes, contamination, and other potential hazards. For example, federal facilities that manage hazardous wastes or underground storage tanks are subject to closure requirements similar to private industrial facilities. If contamination is present, remediation may be required to prevent potentially harmful exposures subsequent to transfer. Some federal facilities also may contain more unique hazards, such as unexploded ordnance on DOD installations or radiological wastes from the past production of nuclear weapons at Department of Energy (DOE) facilities. Federal facilities not involved in industrial operations still may contain hazardous substances from other sources that could present challenges for transfer and reuse, such as asbestos or lead-based paint in buildings. In addition to human health and safety hazards, the potential impacts of a transfer on certain natural or cultural resources (such as historic buildings) also must be assessed. How such resources would be protected by the recipient of a federal property subsequent to transfer may be a potential issue.

The time and resources necessary for compliance with environmental and historical requirements may vary considerably among individual properties depending on applicability. The process of determining which federal requirements may apply and how compliance must be demonstrated is sometimes referred to as the environmental review process (or environmental and historical review). Actions necessary to complete the review process are generally integrated into the broader due diligence process established in federal regulation, during which the landholding agency would be required to assess and determine various details about the property, such as[52]

- any past activities or present conditions at the site that could pose a human health or safety hazard—the existence of mold hazards, radon hazards, asbestos-containing materials, or lead-based paint in any building; whether pesticides have been applied in the management of the property; or whether past activities at the site resulted in the release of hazardous substances that must be remediated;
- the property's location—in a federally designated floodplain, wetland, or coastal zone; or in an area that contains federally threatened or endangered species; and
- the property's historical significance—a site, buildings or fixtures on the site that are historically, architecturally, or culturally significant.

For each criterion, at a minimum, the landholding agency would be required to evaluate the property to determine whether or not such conditions or issues exist. Depending on that evaluation, the agency may be required to comply with certain environmental laws, regulations, or executive orders before they can make a final decision regarding the disposition of the property. Certain federal requirements may apply specifically because the property disposition would involve a transfer from federal ownership. That is, the disposition may be subject to certain requirements that generally would not apply (or could apply differently) to property transfers between nonfederal agencies or private entities. The principal federal statutes that govern the environmental review process, identification and remediation of hazardous substances, and historic preservation are outlined below, followed by a summary of the requirements of each statute. Other federal and state laws also may apply to a property transfer depending on the site-specific conditions.

- The National Environmental Protection Act (NEPA; 42 U.S.C. §§4321 et seq.). Under NEPA, federal agencies must consider the environmental impacts of an action before making a final decision about that action. With regard to surplus property disposal, the responsible federal agency would be required to identify impacts associated with both reporting the property as excess and disposal of the property, but not necessarily its future development that would not constitute a federal action itself.
- The Comprehensive Environmental Response, Compensation, and Liability Act of 1980 (CERCLA; 42 U.S.C. §§9601 et seq.). Section 120(h) of CERCLA generally requires federal agencies to clean up contaminated federal property prior to transferring the property out of federal ownership, unless assurances are provided that the cleanup will be carried out subsequent to transfer and certain conditions are satisfied. To ensure compliance with CERCLA, a federal agency would be required to certify whether or not hazardous substance activity took place during the period of federal ownership and whether, as a result, hazardous substances were released that may warrant remediation.
- The National Historic Preservation Act (NHPA; 16 U.S.C. §§470 et seq.). Section 106 of NHPA requires any federal agency with jurisdiction over a proposed federal undertaking to take into account the effect that the undertaking will have on any district, site, building, structure, or object that is included in or eligible for inclusion in the National Register of Historic Places (i.e., a property significant in American history, architecture, archaeology, engineering, or culture).

Some level of compliance with NEPA and CERCLA generally would be required for all federal agency actions related to the closure and disposal of federal surplus property, at least to document whether there would be any significant environmental impacts with respect to NEPA and whether hazardous substances may be present with respect to CERCLA. Compliance with NHPA would be required if the property being disposed is included or eligible for inclusion in the National Register or if its disposal would affect such a property. Within the framework of documenting any environmental impacts associated with the property disposal, under NEPA, the responsible agency would incorporate information on how compliance with CERCLA would be demonstrated and whether compliance with any other laws, such as NHPA, would be required.

The National Environmental Policy Act[53]

Signed into law in 1970, NEPA has been interpreted as having two primary goals—to ensure that federal agencies consider the environmental impacts of their actions *before* a final decision is made about the action, and to require those agencies to inform the public of those impacts. As a procedural statute, NEPA is intended to inform a federal agency's decision-making process, but does not require that agency to elevate environmental concerns above others.

Regulations implementing NEPA were promulgated by the Council on Environmental Quality (CEQ).[54] Those regulations identify actions subject to NEPA to include those over which a federal agency[55] has some control or responsibility.[56] For example, NEPA may apply to federal agency decisions on the adoption of agency plans and the approval of specific projects. That is, any planning decision or approval that must be made by the landholding agency regarding surplus property disposal may be subject to some level of review under NEPA.

For non-BRAC properties, agency actions subject to NEPA generally include those related to decisions regarding the (1) closure of the facility and reporting it as excess; and (2) disposition of the property.[57] After it accepts a property for disposal from another federal agency, GSA takes responsibility for completing the NEPA process for any subsequent disposal-related activities. However, the landholding agency would be required to complete any necessary NEPA review for actions that pertain to its decision to report the property as excess.

While multiple actions related to surplus property disposal may be subject to NEPA, the analysis required to document compliance is usually limited. The most extensive level of analysis, the preparation of an environmental impact statement (EIS), is rarely required for surplus property disposal. An EIS is required for actions that will significantly affect the quality of the human environment.[58] Among other requirements, it must identify and analyze any impacts of the proposal and identify all reasonable alternatives to the proposal, as well as the impacts of those alternatives. With the exception of federal actions undertaken as part of the BRAC process, federal real property disposal rarely involves significant environmental impacts.

For federal real estate transactions, significant impacts generally occur (i.e., the preparation of an EIS may be required) when the action is likely to involve major new construction. That may be the case when a federal agency is buying property for development, but not generally when disposing of a property. While a property transferred from federal ownership may be further developed, the landholding agency is not required to determine how a potential buyer may use the property before making a decision to dispose of it. Often property disposal involves the disposition of a property that has already been developed. Implementing the BRAC process, however, involves the closure of one military property and the potential expansion of another. As a result, decisions implementing the BRAC process have been those most likely to require the preparation of an EIS.

Regardless of whether an EIS would be required, agencies are obligated to identify the potential impacts of the disposition to ensure that it would not have significant impacts. If the impact of the proposed disposition is uncertain, an agency may ensure compliance with NEPA by preparing an environmental assessment (EA). The result would be either a decision to prepare an EIS or to issue a finding of no significant impacts (FONSI).[59] NEPA compliance may also be documented as part of a categorical exclusion (CATEX) determination.[60] A CATEX is applied to actions that individual agencies have determined, based on their experiences with similar actions in the past, have no individually or cumulatively significant effect on the environment.[61] CEQ allows an action to be processed as a CATEX as long as it involves no extraordinary circumstances that could result in significant impacts.

Each federal agency's procedures to implement NEPA[62] explicitly list actions likely to be approved as a CE or, under certain conditions, an EA. For example GSA's NEPA procedures identify specific actions that can demonstrate compliance with NEPA by completing a "CATEX checklist."[63] That checklist is used to ensure that a given action would involve no extraordinary circumstances that would result in significant environmental impacts. Included among such action, GSA explicitly identifies property disposal actions undertaken for another federal agency, where that agency has already documented compliance with applicable legal requirements such as NEPA, NHPA, and CERCLA; and disposal of real property required by public law wherein Congress has not specifically exempted the action from the requirements of NEPA.[64]

A determination that the disposal of surplus federal property would result in no significant impacts, under NEPA, is not equivalent to determining that the disposition would result in no regulated impacts. For example, if a federal property is listed on the National Register of Historic Places, the impact of its disposition may be deemed insignificant, but only if there are certain restrictions placed on the future use or development of the property. Within the context of ensuring compliance with NEPA, the landholding agency may be required to identify measures necessary to ensure future protection of the resource. In this instance, the requirement to protect that resource could originate with the NHPA (or any other applicable law intended to protect cultural, archaeological, or historical resources), not NEPA. Still, the NEPA compliance process may not be complete until decisions have been made regarding how the landholding agency will ensure compliance with those other applicable laws.

As noted above, one of NEPA's primary goals is to inform the public of the environmental impacts of a proposed action. CEQ regulations implementing NEPA specify public involvement requirements that apply primarily to actions that require an EIS. However, individual agencies have determined that public participation may also be appropriate in the preparation of an EA/FONSI or when determining whether the action may involve some exceptional circumstances that would prevent the application of a CATEX. Each agency has discretion in determining the level and kind of public participation required for such actions. For surplus property disposal, the level of public participation will likely depend on the nature of property itself and the potential public interest in that property's potential closure and disposition.

There may be public opposition to the closure and disposition of surplus federal property. The reasons for such opposition will be unique to that property. However, opposition could arise if there is public concern that future development of the land would no longer be subject to certain federal requirements. For example, after the property transfers from federal ownership (e.g., to a local or state agency or to a private developer), the impacts of future development would generally not be subject to federal agency review or public comment under NEPA or NHPA. Another example of such a law is the Archeological and Historical Preservation Act (AHPA). It requires federal agencies to identify and recover data from archeological sites threatened by their actions. Since a nonfederal land owner would not be required to take such action, members of the public may want the landholding agency to ensure that the property has been adequately surveyed to identify archeological sites or to make the sale conditional on a buyer agreeing to implement certain actions if archeological sites are later discovered.

The Comprehensive Environmental Response, Compensation, and Liability Act[65]

The Comprehensive Environmental Response, Compensation, and Liability Act (CERCLA) is the principal federal statute that addresses releases of hazardous substances into the environment on both federal and nonfederal lands.[66] Section 120(h) of CERCLA generally requires the United States to clean up contaminated federal property prior to transferring the property out of federal ownership.[67] The policy premise of this provision is that the United States should assume full responsibility for the cleanup of contamination caused by federal activities, and not shift the burden of that responsibility to the recipient merely as a consequence of acquiring the property.

Section 120(h) applies to all contaminated federal property declared surplus to the needs of the federal government. The agency with administrative jurisdiction over a surplus federal property generally is responsible for performing and paying for the cleanup of contamination to fulfill the financial liability of the United States. In some cases, the recipient may voluntarily agree to pay for the cleanup of a contaminated surplus federal property in exchange for a discounted purchase price to acquire the property, or other conditions of ownership that the recipient may desire.

As is the case with federal facilities that remain in federal ownership, funds available for the cleanup of surplus federal properties are subject to the availability of appropriations to the federal agencies that administer those properties. For example, the Department of Defense (DOD) performs and pays for the cleanup of surplus federal property on military installations closed under a consolidated Base Realignment and Closure (BRAC) round out of funds appropriated to the DOD Base Closure Account. Federal facilities generally are not eligible for cleanup funds appropriated to the Environmental Protection Agency (EPA) under the Superfund program, which addresses nonfederal sites elevated for priority federal attention. However, EPA oversees the cleanup of federal facilities through the Superfund program in conjunction with the states, in a manner similar to the enforcement of cleanup liability at nonfederal sites. At federal facilities, the administering federal agency serves as the responsible party on behalf of the United States.

Section 120(h) of CERCLA does not bind the United States to cleaning up a surplus federal property for any one particular land use. As a result, the reuse of a property is negotiated between the administering federal agency and the recipient of the property. Disagreements over reuse can arise if the recipient intends to use the property for a purpose that would necessitate a level of cleanup that the federal agency may consider too costly, relative to available appropriations to fund the cleanup. The capabilities of cleanup technologies also could constrain the reuse of a surplus federal property, if it would be impractical to achieve a level of cleanup that would be needed to make the property suitable for a use that the recipient may desire.

Continuing Liability of the United States

Consistent with the policy premise of Section 120(h) of CERCLA and retroactive liability under Section 107[68] of the statute, the United States remains responsible for contamination found not to have been sufficiently remediated after the property is transferred out of federal ownership. Section 120(h)(3) requires the continuing liability of the United States to be specified through a "covenant" incorporated into the deed transferring the property out of federal ownership.[69] The covenant must warrant that all remedial actions necessary to protect human health and the environment have been taken before the date of transfer, and that the United States shall conduct any additional remedial actions found to be necessary after the date of transfer. A clause also must be included in the deed granting the United States access to the property to perform cleanup actions for which it may be responsible.

In practice, the contents of a deed can place certain limitations on the continuing responsibility of the United States. A deed to a transferred federal property typically warrants cleanup only to a level suitable for the land use negotiated prior to transfer. In some cases, a deed may include a restriction prohibiting certain uses that would be considered unsuitable relative to the level of cleanup performed by the United States. Under such deed restrictions, the United States typically assumes responsibility for additional cleanup only to the extent that more work is found to be needed to make the originally agreed-upon use suitable.

If the new owner later decides to use the property for a different purpose, the new owner typically must assume responsibility for the additional cleanup costs to make the property suitable for the desired purpose. In some instances, a deed may prohibit certain land uses even if the new owner is willing to pay the cleanup costs. For example, a deed to a decommissioned military training range may prohibit residential or other land uses because of limitations on cleanup technologies to detect and remove unexploded ordnance. Cleanup capabilities may be constrained especially when ordnance is located beneath the surface, or concealed on the surface by dense vegetation.

Transfer of Uncontaminated Parcels

Some surplus federal properties may contain a mix of contaminated and uncontaminated parcels of land. Although the clean parcels may be ready for reuse, the requirement to clean up the contaminated parcels under Section 120(h) of CERCLA prior to transfer could delay the conveyance of the property as a whole. To address such situations, the 102nd Congress enacted the Community Environmental Response Facilitation Act (CERFA; P.L. 102-426) in 1992. This law amended Section 120(h) by adding a new subsection (4) that authorizes the transfer of uncontaminated parcels on a surplus federal property while cleanup continues on the contaminated parcels.[70] This parcel-by-parcel approach is intended to avoid potential delays in the transfer of "clean" surplus federal lands for reuse, especially such lands on closed military installations where economic redevelopment is desired to replace lost jobs. In the event that previously unknown contamination is later discovered after transfer out of federal ownership, Section 120(h)(4)(D) requires that a deed to an uncontaminated parcel still include a covenant warranting that the United States shall conduct cleanup actions that may become necessary to address contamination attributed to past federal activities.[71]

Early Transfer of Contaminated Parcels

The cleanup of a contaminated parcel may take several years or more, depending on the type and level of contamination, technical feasibility of cleanup actions, and availability of appropriations to pay for the cleanup. In such situations, the requirement to complete cleanup prior to transfer out of federal ownership could result in delaying the transfer. Enacted in the 104th Congress, Section 334 of the National Defense Authorization Act for FY1997 (P.L. 104-201) amended Section 120(h)(3) of CERCLA to add a new subsection (C) that allows the transfer of a contaminated parcel on a surplus federal property before cleanup is complete, if certain conditions are satisfied.[72] Although Congress enacted this amendment in annual defense authorization legislation, this authority applies to any surplus federal property administered by any federal agency, not just surplus U.S. military property.

Section 120(h)(3)(C) specifically authorizes a deferral of the cleanup covenant to allow the transfer of title to a contaminated parcel on a surplus federal property before cleanup is complete. Federal agencies often refer to this deferral of the covenant as an "early" transfer, although the statute does not use this term. The deed to a contaminated property transferred out of federal ownership must contain assurances that the cleanup still will be carried out after the property leaves federal ownership. The federal agency responsible for the performance of the cleanup also must identify the funding needed to carry out the cleanup in its annual budget requests.

The deed also must restrict the use of the property to purposes that would be protective of human health and environment, while the cleanup proceeds. For example, at the time of transfer, a property may be suitable for industrial use because the risks of exposure to contamination may be within an acceptable range, whereas other land uses that would result in potentially harmful exposure would be restricted until the property is cleaned up sufficiently for that purpose. Once cleanup is complete, the United States remains obligated to provide a covenant at that time, warranting that all necessary actions to protect human health and the environment have been taken to make the property suitable for its intended, eventual use.

The early transfer of a contaminated surplus federal property that EPA has designated on the National Priorities List (NPL) for cleanup purposes is subject to the concurrence of the Administrator of EPA and the governor of the state in which the facility is located. The early transfer of a contaminated surplus federal property that is not listed on the NPL still requires the concurrence of the governor of the state in which the facility is located, but not EPA. Federal agencies proposing an early transfer also must provide the public at least 30 days advance notice and an opportunity to comment on the proposed transfer before it is executed.

National Historic Preservation Act[73]

When federal property is sold, a review under the National Historic Preservation Act[74] (NHPA) may be required to determine whether the action will adversely affect historic properties and how to mitigate those effects. Courts describe NHPA as a "stop, look, and listen" statute that directs an agency to consider the effects of its action on historic sites, but does not require an agency to stop a project that would harm that property.[75] Instead, NHPA requires an agency to make an informed determination following a decision making process that is known as a Section 106 review.[76]

Federal agencies conduct a Section 106 review when their actions, known as *undertakings*, may affect a historic property. An *undertaking* is defined as "a project, activity, or program funded in whole or in part under the direct or indirect jurisdiction of a Federal agency."[77] The Section 106 process begins before federal funding is provided or a federal license issued.[78] Starting a Section 106 review early in the project development process ensures that agencies consider "a broad range of alternatives" during the planning process.[79]

When a federal agency finds an action is an undertaking, its first step is to identify the parties required to be involved in the decision making process, who are known as *consulting* parties. NHPA regulations define who must be invited as a consulting party,[80] including the State Historic Preservation Officer (SHPO), the Tribal Historic Preservation Officer (THPO), local and tribal officials, and, if the federal undertaking involves issuing a permit, the applicant. Other *interested* parties may participate, such as historic associations and general members of the public, but do not have the same standing in the decision making process as the consulting parties.[81]

Next, the agency identifies the area of potential effects (APE), defined as "the geographic area or areas within which an undertaking may directly or indirectly cause alterations in the character or use of historic properties."[82] At this stage, the action agency, with the consulting parties, identifies historic properties that may be affected. Historic properties are defined as those listed or eligible for listing in the National Register of Historic Places.[83] If no historic properties are within the APE, the Section106 process concludes.

When historic properties are found within the APE, the agency will coordinate with the consulting parties to determine whether the undertaking will adversely affect the property. If no adverse effects are found, the Section 106 process ends. The undertaking does not have to touch a historic property physically for an agency to find an adverse effect, as the NHPA regulations state that the agency must consider both direct and indirect effects of the project,[84] as well as reasonably foreseeable effects that may occur later in time or at some distance, or are cumulative.[85] Accordingly, NHPA would apply not only to selling federally owned historic buildings but may also apply when the sale of a non-historic building would adversely affect historic properties. For example, if the sale of a non-historic federal building could change the character of a historic area, that might be considered an adverse effect and would require further analysis.

If adverse effects on historic properties are found, NHPA does not require the agency to reject the undertaking. Instead, the agency is required to compile adequate documentation of its adverse effects findings, make the documentation available to the public, and provide an opportunity for comment.[86] An additional consulting party may be invited at this stage—the Advisory Council on Historic Places (ACHP or the Council).[87] The agency, with the cooperation of the consulting parties, shall "develop and evaluate alternatives or modifications to the undertaking that could avoid, minimize, or mitigate adverse effects on historic properties."[88] When the parties agree on avoidance and/or mitigation of the adverse effects, the agency and the SHPO/THPO will enter into a binding agreement known as a Memorandum of Agreement (MOA),[89] and consulting parties are invited to concur.[90] Completion of a MOA concludes the Section 106 process.

If the parties cannot reach an agreement on the adverse effects, the agency, the SHPO/THPO, or the Council may terminate the Section 106 process.[91] The terminating party must notify the others in writing of the basis for ending consultation, and the ACHP will provide the opportunity for the parties (including itself) and the public to comment. However, termination of the Section 106 process does not mean that the project must also be terminated. If the agency decides to continue the undertaking, the agency must document its rationale and demonstrate that it considered the comments of the Council.[92] The agency must give a copy of this document to the consulting parties and make it available to the public.[93] Then, the agency may advance its project despite any harm to historic properties, taking any mitigation measures it chooses.

End Notes

[1] Federal Real Property Council, FY2013 Federal Real Property Report: An Overview of the U.S. Federal Government's Real Property Assets, August 2014, p. 1.

[2] U.S. Government Accountability Office, Federal Real Property: Progress Made in Reducing Unneeded Property, but VA Needs Better Information to Make Further Reductions, GAO-08-939, September 2008, p. 9.

[3] U.S. Government Accountability Office, Federal Real Property: Excess and Underutilized Property is an Ongoing Problem, GAO-06-248, February 2006, p. 3. For more information, see CRS Report R40476, Base Realignment and Closure (BRAC): Transfer and Disposal of Military Property, by R. Chuck Mason.

[4] Federal Real Property Council, FY2013 Federal Real Property Report: An Overview of the U.S. Federal Government's Real Property Assets, August 2014, p. 15.

[5] This section was written by Garrett Hatch, Specialist in American National Government, x7-7822.

[6] 40 U.S.C. §101 et. seq. Land reserved for national forest or national park purposes, and Bureau of Land Management properties, are not covered by these disposal rules. Other legislation that governs federal agency real property disposal includes the National Historic Preservation Act (16 U.S.C. §470 et. seq.), which establishes guidelines for agency disposition of historic properties, and the Stewart B. McKinney Homeless Assistance Act (42 U.S.C. §11411), which requires agencies to make surplus real property available first for homeless use before making it available for other purposes. In addition, Executive Order 13327, signed in 2004 by President George W. Bush, established (1) Senior Real Property Officers (SRPOs) at 24 of the largest landholding agencies to monitor and manage their agencies' real property, (2) a Federal Real Property Council, comprised of SRPOs, to evaluate agency real property policies and practices, and (3) the Federal Real Property Profile, a database with information on agency real property holdings, including disposition data.

[7] The Department of Defense has the authority to dispose of unneeded real property that is subject to the Base Realignment and Closure (BRAC) process, but GSA disposes of non-BRAC real property. The U.S. Postal Service has the authority to dispose of all of its real property. The Departments of State, Veterans Affairs, Education, Health and Human Services, the Interior, and Agriculture also have the authority to dispose of some unneeded real property, although the scope of that authority varies widely.

[8] 40 U.S.C. §102.

[9] U.S. General Services Administration, Customer Guide to Real Property Disposal, p. 17, at http://www.missionumatilla.com/documents/historical_data/HD0013_PropertyDisposalClosureGuide_GSA.pdf.

[10] The Office of Real Property Utilization and Disposal website address is https://extportal.pbs.gsa.gov/ ResourceCenter/viewproperties.do?noticetype=1.

[11] Only the 24 federal agencies are required to report their real property data annually to the FRPP, although other agencies have the option of reporting. The agencies that are required to report are the Departments of Agriculture, Commerce, Defense, Education, Energy, Health and Human Services, Homeland Security, Housing and Urban Development, the Interior, Justice, Labor, State, Transportation, the Treasury, and Veterans Affairs; Environmental Protection Agency; General Services Administration; National Aeronautics and Space Administration; National Science Foundation; Nuclear Regulatory Commission; Office of Personnel Management; Small Business Administration; Social Security Administration; and United States Agency for International Development.

[12] See 41 C.F.R. §102-75.1275; 41 C.F.R. §§102-75.190-102-75.225; and 40 U.S.C. §522. When an agency is required to pay fair market value for a property, the government does not realize any new revenue since the funds are being transferred from another federal agency.

[13] 40 U.S.C. §102.

[14] 40 U.S.C. §549.

[15] 40 U.S.C. §550. The agencies that sponsor conveyances are the Departments of Education (education), Health and Human Services (public health, homeless services), the Interior (parks and recreation, historic monuments, wildlife conservation), Justice (correctional), Transportation (port facility), Housing and Urban Development (housing), Justice (law

enforcement), Homeland Security (emergency management response), and the Federal Aviation Authority (public airports).

[16] 42 U.S.C. 11411.

[17] 41 C.F.R. §102-75.1200.

[18] Conveyances, other than McKinney Act transfers, are at the discretion of the agency and are not required by statute.

[19] U.S. General Services Administration, Surplus Real Property Available for Public Use: Notification Procedure, GSA website, at http://www.gsa.gov/Portal/gsa/ep/contentView.do?contentType=GSA_BASIC&contentId=20146.

[20] U.S. General Services Administration, Customer Guide to Real Property, p. 25. The General Services Administration is responsible for deeding, conveyance, and compliance monitoring of correctional, law enforcement, and emergency management conveyances, and for just deeding and conveyance of properties to be used for historic monuments, or public airports.

[21] 41 C.F.R. §102-75.880(d); 40 U.S.C. §545.

[22] Ibid.

[23] U.S. General Services Administration, Office of Real Property Utilization and Disposal, "How to Acquire Federal Property," at https://extportal.pbs.gsa.gov/ResourceCenter/content/acquireFedProp.do.

[24] General Services Administration, Office of Real Property Utilization and Disposal, Current Sales webpage, at https://extportal.pbs.gsa.gov/ResourceCenter/PRHomePage/ loadPRHomePage.do?type=full.

[25] General Services Administration, Customer Guide to Real Property Disposal, p. 27.

[26] Federal Real Property Council, FY2013 Federal Real Property Report: An Overview of the U.S. Federal Government's Real Property Assets, August 2014, p. 1.

[27] This section was prepared by Garrett Hatch, Specialist in American National Government.

[28] Thus, for example, Congress exempted USPS from the federal property disposition statutes (40 U.S.C. §101).

[29] 39 U.S.C. 401(5).

[30] P.L. 91-375; 84 Stat. 725 (39 U.S.C. §101 et seq.)

[31] 39 U.S.C. 201. With the PRA, Congress relinquished a great deal of control over USPS's operations as that control had proven problematic. Congressional directives often inhibited the Post Office Department from controlling its operating costs and increasing its prices.

[32] 39 U.S.C. §403(b).

[33] 39 U.S.C. §404(a)(13).

[34] Over the past century, the proportion of mail sorted by postal workers has greatly declined with the advent of machinery that can read the addresses on letters and parcels and sort them according to their destination.

[35] U.S. Postal Service, U.S. Postal Service Facilities Guide to Real Property Acquisitions and Related Services, Handbook RE-1, October 2008, p. 15, at https://about.usps.com/handbooks/re1.pdf.

[36] For example, see http://www.uspspropertiesforsale.com/.

[37] Staff, "Let the Bidding Begin," Chicago Tribune, August 27, 2009, at http://articles.chicagotribune.com/2009-08-27/ news/0908260669_1_condos-minimum-bid-requirement-real-estate.

[38] 39 U.S.C. 404(d); and 39 C.F.R. 241, "Post Office Organization and Administration: Establishment, Classification, and Discontinuance," at 76 F.R. 41413-41424, July 14, 2011

[39] 39 U.S.C. 404(d) sets the PRC's role in the appeals process.

[40] For a more detailed description of the post office closure process, see CRS Report R41950, The U.S. Postal Service: Common Questions About Post Office Closures, by Kevin R. Kosar, pp. 6-7.

[41] This section was prepared by Daniel H. Else, Specialist in National Defense.

[42] See 10 U.S.C. 2687 note.

[43] State and local governments and certain nonprofit organizations may qualify for a public benefits conveyance of surplus public property at reduced or no cost for a number of specified uses.

[44] So-called BRAC rounds were carried out in 1988, 1991, 1993, 1995, and 2005. The 1988 round was authorized by Defense Authorization Amendments and Base Closure and Realignment Act (P.L. 100-526, §1, 102 Stat. 2623). The 1991, 1993, and 1995 rounds were authorized by the Defense Base Closure and Realignment Act of 1990 (part A of Title XXIX of P.L. 101-510). Both acts were codified in 10 U.S.C. 2687 note. The 2005 round was created in a reauthorization of the 1990 law enacted in the National Defense Authorization Act for Fiscal Year 2002 (P.L. 107-107, Division A, Title X, Subtitle E, §1048(d)(2), Division B, Title XXVIII, Subtitle C, §2821(b), Title XXX, §§3001-3007, 115 Stat. 1227, 1312, 1342).

[45] Defense Base Closure and Realignment Act of 1990, as amended, Section 2912(a)(1)(A).

[46] Ibid., Section 2912(a)(1)(B).

[47] Ibid., Section 2913.

[48] The President has not yet disapproved any commission's recommendation list.

[49] For more information on joint resolutions, see CRS Report 98-728, Bills, Resolutions, Nominations, and Treaties: Characteristics, Requirements, and Uses, by Richard S. Beth and CRS Report 98-706, Bills and Resolutions: Examples of How Each Kind Is Used, by Richard S. Beth. Though resolutions have been introduced in one chamber or the other during every BRAC round, none has survived its initial floor vote.

[50] The Secretary's Office of Economic Adjustment has served as the principal organization through which such assistance has been offered.

[51] An overview of environmental requirements that may apply to the transfer of surplus federal property is available in the General Services Administration (GSA) "Environmental Framework for Real Property Disposal" at http://propertydisposal.gsa.gov/ Environmen talInfo.

[52] GSA regulations identifying the information required from federal departments and agencies for property declared excess to their needs are codified at 41 C.F.R. Part 102-75, Subpart B. The criteria that must be evaluated under these regulations before GSA will accept a property for disposal also are identified in GSA's "Excess Real Property Checklist" (available at http://propertydisposal.gsa.gov/FAA). The checklist is a supplement to its "Standard Form 118, Report of Excess Real Property." When the Postal Service, DOD, and DOD agencies dispose of their own excess real property, each agency is required to evaluate similar criteria.

[53] This section was prepared by Linda Luther, Analyst in Environmental Policy.

[54] 40 C.F.R. Parts 1500-1508.

[55] "Federal agencies" are defined at 40 C.F.R. §1508.12 to include all agencies of the federal government, but not Congress, the Judiciary, or the President.

[56] 40 C.F.R. §1508.18.

[57] Congress, not individual military agencies, identifies military bases that are subject to closure as part of the BRAC process. As a result, base closure decisions are not subject to NEPA. However, the military agency responsible for the base closure may have a certain degree of

discretion in implementing the closure, as well as the action that must be taken to realign the activities at the closing base with another facility. Actions taken to implement the base closure are subject to NEPA.

[58] As required at 42 U.S.C. §4322(2)(C). In accordance with the CEQ regulations, the significance of a proposal's impacts are determined on a case-by-case basis depending on the context and intensity of those impacts (see 40 C.F.R. §1508.27). Also, CEQ defines the "human environment" to include the natural and physical environment and the relationship of people with that environment (see 40 C.F.R. §1508.13).

[59] See 40 C.F.R. §§1501.3 and 1508.9.

[60] CATEXs are referred to as such because they are actions that are categorically excluded from the requirement to prepare an EIS or EA.

[61] See 40 C.F.R. §1508.4

[62] Each federal agency was required to adopt the CEQ regulations implementing NEPA and to supplement them with procedures necessary to implement NEPA that are relevant to the action undertaken by that agency. GSA, USPS, and DOD, as well as each of agency within DOD, have done so.

[63] See the "PBS National Environmental Policy Act NEPA Desk Guide," October 1999, Section 5.4 Checklist CATEXs. The NEPA Desk Guide is available at http://www.gsa.gov/nepadeskguide.

[64] See the GSA's NEPA Desk Guide, Sections 5.4(c) and (g).

[65] This section was prepared by David M. Bearden, Specialist in Environmental Policy.

[66] 42 U.S.C. §9601 et seq. For a broader discussion of CERCLA, see CRS Report R41039, Comprehensive Environmental Response, Compensation, and Liability Act: A Summary of Superfund Cleanup Authorities and Related Provisions of the Act, by David M. Bearden.

[67] 42 U.S.C. §9620(h).

[68] 42 U.S.C. §9607.

[69] 42 U.S.C. §9620(h)(3).

[70] 42 U.S.C. §9620(h)(4).

[71] 42 U.S.C. §9620(h)(4)(D).

[72] 42 U.S.C. §9620(h)(3)(C).

[73] This section was prepared by Kristina Alexander, Legislative Attorney.

[74] P.L. 89-665, 80 Stat. 915; 16 U.S.C. §§470 et seq.

[75] See Safeguarding the Historic Hanscom Area's Irreplaceable Resources, Inc. v. Federal Aviation Administration, 651 F.3d 202, 214 (1st Cir. 2011); Business and Residents Alliance of East Harlem v. Jackson, 430 F.3d 584, 591 (2d Cir. 2005); Muckleshoot Indian Tribe v. U.S. Forest Service, 177 F.3d 800, 805 (9th Cir. 1999); Illinois Commerce Commission v. Interstate Commerce Commission, 848 F.2d 1246, 1261 (D.C. Cir. 1988).

[76] It is named after the section within the public law enacting NHPA, P.L. 89-665, §106, but is codified at 16 U.S.C. §470f.

[77] 16 U.S.C. §470w(7); 36 C.F.R. §800.16(y).

[78] 16 U.S.C. §470f.

[79] 36 C.F.R. §800.1(c).

[80] 36 C.F.R. §800.2(a)(4).

[81] For example, the agency is not required to confer with interested parties, unlike consulting parties, on key issues such as resolving any adverse effects, as discussed later in this section.

[82] 36 C.F.R. §800.16(d).

[83] 36 C.F.R. §800.4.

[84] 36 C.F.R. §800.16(d).
[85] 36 C.F.R. §800.5(a)(1).
[86] 36 C.F.R. §800.6(a)(4).
[87] The ACHP is an independent federal agency. It is required to be invited to participate in developing an MOA under three circumstances: if a National Historic Landmark will be adversely affected (36 C.F.R. §800.6(a)(1)); if a programmatic agreement affecting multiple agency undertakings is being prepared (36 C.F.R. §800.6(a)(1)); or if the parties fail to come to terms on a MOA (36 C.F.R. §800.6(b)(1)(v)).
[88] 36 C.F.R. §800.6(a).
[89] 36 C.F.R. §800.6(c)(1).
[90] 36 C.F.R. §800.6(c)(3).
[91] 36 C.F.R. §800.7.
[92] 36 C.F.R. §800.7(c)(4).
[93] 36 C.F.R. §800.7(c)(4).

INDEX

A

access, viii, 2, 14, 18, 40, 44, 45, 47, 48, 56, 107
accountability, 42, 43, 83
accounting, 55, 60, 61, 75, 76, 83
acquisitions, ix, 22, 30, 44, 60, 61, 62, 63, 67, 68, 69, 70, 78, 79, 81, 82, 83, 84, 85, 86, 87, 88
adjustment, 46, 100
adverse effects, 110, 111, 115
advocacy, 54
Afghanistan, 67
agency actions, 103
agency decisions, 103
Agricultural Research Service (ARS), 19, 22
Air Force, 96
airports, 93, 113
American Recovery and Reinvestment Act, 28, 55
American Recovery and Reinvestment Act of 2009, 28, 55
appraisals, 75, 80, 88
appraised value, 30, 94
appropriations, vii, viii, 1, 4, 5, 18, 24, 27, 29, 31, 35, 41, 44, 45, 46, 47, 48, 52, 53, 95, 106, 107, 108
Appropriations Act, 87
approval process, viii, 2, 4, 6, 7, 9
ARS, 17, 19, 35, 38, 40
asbestos, 39, 101
assessment, 14, 41, 43, 52, 57, 98, 104
assets, 25, 26, 27, 34, 42, 43, 45, 49, 52, 54, 55, 57, 61, 66, 77, 90, 92
audit(s), 7, 12, 23, 64, 86
authority(s), vii, viii, ix, x, 1, 3, 4, 5, 6, 18, 19, 20, 22, 26, 27, 31, 32, 38, 39, 40, 41, 44, 47, 48, 49, 50, 51, 55, 56, 57, 60, 64, 89, 90, 91, 94, 95, 97, 98, 100, 109, 112
autonomy, x, 90, 94
avoidance, 31, 39, 43, 49, 50, 78, 111

B

balance sheet, 55
banks, 56
barriers, 19, 32
base, 23, 91, 96, 100, 114
Beijing, 69
benchmarks, 88
benefits, x, 19, 23, 40, 42, 49, 53, 57, 90, 114
Bolivia, 80
bonds, 47
Bosnia, 64, 85
bounds, 19, 41
Brazil, 69, 73, 87
Budget Committee, 25
budget resolution, 25, 56

Bureau of Land Management, 112
Bush, George W., 112
Bush, President George W., 112
businesses, ix, 89, 91, 95
buyer(s), 32, 40, 104, 106

C

cables, 88
CAF, 17, 49, 50, 52, 57
capital projects, 36
case study(s), ix, 18, 21, 22, 30, 60, 64, 86
cash, 35, 37
CERCLA, x, 90, 102, 103, 105, 106, 107, 108, 115
certification, 99
chain of command, 97
challenges, 18, 19, 23, 29, 32, 40, 42, 47, 52, 53, 56, 64, 70, 73, 75, 86, 101
Chicago, 96, 113
Chief of Staff, 40, 53
China, 69
cities, 64
Civilian Property Realignment Act, viii, 2, 15, 23
civilization, 24
classification, 85
cleaning, 107
cleanup, 32, 39, 102, 106, 107, 108, 109
clients, 6
closure, 23, 96, 99, 100, 101, 103, 104, 105, 114
Cold War, 91, 98
collaboration, 48
commercial, 27, 75
community(s), 40, 54, 98, 99, 100
compensation, 97
competition, 46
competitive process, 8
complement, 49, 51
compliance, 31, 80, 101, 102, 103, 104, 105, 113
compounds, 67
Comprehensive Environmental Response, Compensation, and Liability Act (CERCLA), 102, 106, 115
Comprehensive Environmental Response, Compensation, and Liability Act of 1980, 102
computer, 5
conference, 8, 9, 87
conflict, 42
Congress, viii, 1, 2, 3, 4, 5, 6, 7, 9, 11, 12, 13, 15, 18, 19, 20, 21, 22, 24, 25, 27, 31, 38, 41, 42, 44, 46, 48, 49, 50, 52, 53, 63, 65, 69, 84, 86, 87, 88, 89, 95, 97, 98, 99, 105, 108, 113, 114
Congressional Budget Office, 17, 23
conservation, 93, 97
Consolidated Appropriations Act, 87
consolidation, 24, 31, 48
construction, ix, 3, 4, 5, 6, 8, 10, 12, 27, 28, 30, 31, 34, 36, 38, 40, 44, 54, 55, 56, 60, 62, 64, 66, 67, 68, 72, 78, 83, 86, 87, 104
consulting, 110, 111, 115
consumption, 46
contamination, 100, 106, 107, 108, 109
cooperation, 111
coordination, 40
cost effective option, viii, 2, 28
cost effectiveness, 80
cost saving, 23, 34, 43, 49, 50, 54
cost-benefit analysis, 41
counsel, 88
courthouses, vii, 1, 3, 4, 6, 12
culture, 102
customers, 27, 47
cycles, 40

D

data collection, 54
database, 14, 54, 62, 65, 66, 72, 85, 92, 112
decision makers, 42, 52, 83
decision-making process, ix, 60, 63, 85, 103
deficit, 7, 50, 57
Department of Agriculture, 15, 17, 21
Department of Commerce, 15

Department of Defense, x, 15, 59, 67, 90, 91, 96, 106, 112
Department of Education, 15
Department of Energy, 15, 101
Department of Health and Human Services, 15, 93
Department of Homeland Security, 6, 15
Department of Justice, 15
Department of Labor, 15
Department of the Interior, 15, 17, 18, 21
Department of the Treasury, 19
Department of Transportation, 15
Departments of Agriculture, 53, 112
devolution, 45
diplomacy, 73
direct cost, 37
directives, 85, 113
disaster, 6
disposition, 11, 91, 102, 103, 104, 105, 112, 113
distribution, 56
draft, 53, 84

E

economic development, x, 89, 91, 94
education, 112
efficient resource allocation, 28
EIS, 104, 105, 115
embassy, ix, 59, 60, 62, 64, 67, 68, 69, 72, 73, 74, 75, 78, 79, 86, 87
emergency, 6, 113
emergency management, 113
employees, 6
endangered, 101
endangered species, 101
energy, 4, 5, 31, 36, 56
energy efficiency, 5
enforcement, 17, 49, 51, 92, 107
engineering, 102
environment, 104, 106, 107, 109, 115
environmental contamination, 100
environmental factors, 71
environmental impact, 99, 102, 103, 104, 105
environmental impact statement (EIS), 104
Environmental Protection Act, x, 90, 102
Environmental Protection Agency, 15, 106, 112
EPA, x, 90, 102, 106, 109
equipment, 40, 95, 96
erosion, 36
evidence, 8, 22, 23, 64, 82, 86, 88
Excess Federal Building and Property Disposal Act, viii, 2, 15
exclusion, 104
execution, 82
executive branch, 3, 82, 90, 95
executive order(s), 102
exercise, 6
expenditures, 6, 28, 44
expertise, 47, 80, 93
exposure, 109

F

FAA, 114
fair market value, x, 26, 65, 90, 92, 94, 112
FBF, 17, 18, 19, 27, 30, 31, 44, 45, 49, 51, 52, 55, 56
federal agency, x, 11, 27, 90, 92, 93, 97, 102, 103, 104, 105, 107, 109, 110, 112, 115, 116
Federal Buildings Fund, 15, 17, 18, 27, 52, 53, 55, 56
federal facilities, 77, 100, 106
federal government, ix, 3, 20, 23, 24, 32, 33, 34, 35, 54, 56, 78, 81, 83, 87, 89, 94, 100, 106, 111, 112, 113, 114
federal law, 22, 96
federal office space, vii, 1
federal real property, vii, ix, 3, 7, 18, 19, 20, 21, 23, 29, 41, 42, 43, 44, 46, 47, 49, 50, 51, 52, 54, 56, 65, 91, 104
Federal Real Property and Administrative Services Act, x, 89, 91
Federal Real Property Asset Management Reform Act, viii, 2, 15
Federal Register, 93

financial, 11, 20, 27, 31, 32, 39, 40, 52, 54, 55, 74, 77, 82, 83, 106
financial planning, 20
Finland, 64, 85
fiscal policy, 54, 56
flexibility, 19, 38, 41, 42, 43, 44, 45, 48, 52, 78, 79, 87
fluctuations, 78
force, 91, 98, 99
France, 80
freezing, 52
funding, viii, 4, 5, 18, 19, 20, 21, 22, 24, 25, 27, 28, 29, 30, 31, 32, 33, 34, 38, 39, 40, 41, 42, 43, 44, 45, 46, 48, 49, 51, 52, 53, 55, 56, 61, 66, 67, 77, 78, 82, 87, 99, 109, 110
funding mechanisms, ix, 18, 19, 20, 21, 22, 33, 34, 38, 39, 41, 52
funds, 4, 5, 12, 21, 25, 27, 30, 31, 32, 36, 38, 44, 45, 46, 47, 48, 55, 61, 77, 87, 88, 106, 112

G

GAO, ix, 7, 12, 14, 15, 17, 18, 19, 24, 25, 26, 29, 31, 37, 38, 41, 43, 47, 48, 49, 50, 51, 54, 55, 56, 57, 59, 60, 61, 65, 68, 69, 71, 72, 73, 74, 76, 79, 81, 84, 86, 87, 88, 111
General Services Administration (GSA), v, vii, x, 1, 3, 5, 14, 15, 17, 18, 21, 53, 63, 65, 84, 89, 91, 112, 113, 114
government budget, 54, 56
governments, 94
governor, 109
growth, 54, 56, 80
guidance, 22, 25, 43, 60, 61, 65, 66, 67, 77, 80, 81, 82, 83, 84, 85, 87, 88, 94
guidelines, 70, 71, 72, 112

H

hazardous substances, x, 90, 101, 102, 103, 106
hazardous waste(s), 100
hazards, 100, 101
health, 90, 92, 101, 109
Health and Human Services, 112
HHS, 93
historic preservation, x, 54, 90, 91, 102
history, 102
host, 69, 74, 75, 87
House, vii, 1, 4, 8, 15, 25, 62, 97
House Committee on Transportation and Infrastructure, vii, 1, 4, 15
House of Representatives, 62
housing, 4, 37, 38, 62, 78, 79, 80, 86, 87, 88, 112
Housing and Urban Development (HUD), 15, 93, 112
human, 54, 100, 101, 104, 107, 109, 115
human health, 100, 101, 107, 109
human resources, 54
Hungary, 75, 80
Hurricane Katrina, 36, 40

I

identification, x, 41, 57, 90, 96, 98, 102
improvements, 3, 31, 36
income, 27
India, 69, 73
indirect effect, 110
individuals, 23
industry, 5, 23, 42
inflation, 68, 78
information technology, 54
infrastructure, 56, 96
internal processes, 38
Interstate Commerce Commission, 115
investment(s), 8, 21, 28, 32, 42, 43, 45, 52, 53, 65, 78
Iowa, 35, 41
Iraq, 67
issues, vii, 7, 75, 85, 101, 115

J

Jamaica, 77
Japan, 80
judiciary, vii, 1, 3
jurisdiction, 46, 96, 97, 102, 106, 110
justification, viii, 2, 11, 14

K

Kenya, 66

L

land disposal, 35
law enforcement, 113
laws, 20, 31, 41, 98, 102, 103, 105
laws and regulations, 31
lead, 53, 72, 77, 79, 101
lease payments, 26, 30, 31, 33, 34, 37
legislation, x, 3, 9, 14, 23, 25, 26, 36, 48, 50, 90, 109, 112
legislative proposals, 11
lifetime, 26
light, 71
local conditions, 71
local government, ix, x, 11, 35, 54, 56, 89, 90, 91, 92, 93, 94, 114
locus, 45, 49, 51
logistics, 40
Louisiana, 36

M

machinery, 113
maintenance costs, ix, 45, 61, 71, 72, 73, 78, 89
majority, 32, 67
management, ix, 3, 7, 9, 10, 12, 24, 49, 53, 54, 55, 60, 61, 62, 64, 65, 69, 72, 77, 83, 85, 86, 91, 101
manure, 35, 40
marketing, 73, 75, 76, 87
mass, 46, 73
materials, 101
matrix, 66
media, 54
medical, 11, 32, 36
methodology, 64
Mexico, 73
military, 23, 96, 97, 98, 99, 100, 104, 106, 108, 109, 114
mission(s), viii, ix, 6, 18, 19, 30, 32, 33, 42, 43, 44, 45, 64, 73, 77, 79, 89, 90, 96, 98, 99
models, ix, 18, 21
modifications, 111
mold, 101
moratorium, 30

N

Namibia, 77
National Aeronautics and Space Administration, 15, 112
national debt, 91
National Defense Authorization Act, 108, 114
National Historic Preservation Act (NHPA), x, 90, 102, 103, 105, 106, 109, 110, 111, 112, 115
National Park Service, 17, 22
national parks, 90
National Priorities List, 109
national security, 98
National Strategy, 54, 87
natural resources, 100
negotiating, 55, 80
nonprofit organizations, 91, 114
Norton, Eleanor Holmes, 9
NPL, 109
NPS, 17, 22, 34, 36, 38
Nuclear Regulatory Commission, 15, 112
nuclear weapons, 101

O

obstacles, 32
Office of Management and Budget (OMB), 17, 22, 23, 24, 25, 26, 28, 37, 43, 44, 45, 48, 49, 50, 53, 54, 55, 59, 60, 61, 63, 66, 70, 77, 81, 82, 84, 85, 87, 88
officials, ix, 19, 22, 29, 30, 31, 32, 35, 38, 39, 40, 44, 45, 55, 60, 61, 63, 65, 66, 67, 68, 69, 70, 73, 74, 75, 76, 77, 78, 79, 80, 82, 84, 85, 87, 93
omission, 61
operating costs, 70, 71, 76, 77, 87, 91, 113
operations, 5, 28, 31, 44, 45, 81, 96, 98, 99, 101, 113
opportunities, 23, 24, 34, 43, 48, 78
outpatient, 37, 91
oversight, viii, 2, 6, 7, 10, 12, 13, 35, 42, 49, 52, 98
ownership, 28, 30, 34, 55, 71, 78, 82, 102, 104, 105, 106, 107, 108, 109

P

permit, 40, 94, 110
Philippines, 69
physical environment, 115
policy, 9, 12, 24, 25, 73, 91, 93, 95, 106, 107
policy issues, 91
policymakers, 43, 47
population, 95
port of entry, 6
portfolio, vii, ix, 1, 7, 9, 10, 11, 27, 28, 45, 60, 63, 66, 68, 70, 72, 77, 80, 83, 84, 85, 90
ports of entry, vii, 1, 3
potential benefits, 53
PRC, 96, 113
preparation, 32, 33, 71, 104, 105
present value, 26, 28, 30
preservation, x, 32, 54, 90, 91, 102
President, 4, 6, 22, 23, 43, 54, 65, 99, 112, 114
price changes, 51
principles, ix, 18, 19, 22, 42, 54, 56
private sector, 5, 10, 11, 20, 33, 54, 55, 56
procurement, 43, 55
project, vii, viii, 2, 4, 5, 6, 8, 10, 12, 19, 20, 24, 26, 28, 33, 37, 39, 40, 41, 43, 46, 48, 49, 52, 57, 110, 111
Property Act, x, 5, 89, 91
protection, 105
public benefit, x, 11, 90, 92, 93, 94, 97, 100, 114
Public Building Service Savings and Reform Act, viii, 2
public concern, 105
public health, 112
public interest, 105
public-private partnerships, 52

Q

quality assurance, 84
quality control, 85

R

radio, 15
radon, 101
RE, 113
real estate, ix, 23, 24, 60, 62, 72, 75, 79, 80, 88, 95, 96, 104
recognition, 25, 42, 45, 47, 48, 49, 52
recommendations, ix, 18, 42, 53, 60, 62, 72, 84, 99
recovery, 42, 43
recreation, 36, 38, 93, 112
redevelopment, 94, 100, 108
reform(s), viii, 2, 9, 13, 14, 15, 55
regulations, 14, 22, 94, 102, 103, 105, 110, 114, 115
rehabilitation, 93
reliability, 85
remedial actions, 107
remediation, x, 11, 19, 40, 90, 100, 101, 102
renewable energy, 5

renovation projects, ix, 7, 27, 55, 60, 64, 86
rent, viii, 2, 3, 7, 10, 13, 28, 39, 45, 55, 63, 81, 85, 86, 88
rental rate, viii, 2, 9, 13
Reorganization Act, 95
repair, 19, 21, 28, 31, 42, 43, 50, 64, 71, 74, 77
requirements, x, 3, 9, 10, 11, 12, 13, 25, 33, 66, 71, 79, 87, 90, 91, 97, 98, 100, 101, 102, 104, 105, 114
Residential, 74, 79
resolution, 5, 30, 39, 56, 99
resource allocation, 20, 27, 34, 52
resources, viii, 18, 19, 20, 21, 31, 33, 40, 43, 44, 46, 48, 52, 62, 77, 100, 101, 105
response, 53, 54, 66, 85, 113
restrictions, 69, 71, 87, 97, 105, 107
retail, 93
revenue, 25, 44, 47, 61, 62, 63, 77, 85, 95, 112
risk(s), 7, 12, 19, 23, 39, 40, 52, 62, 66, 77, 109
risk assessment, 39
risk management, 39
rules, 25, 26, 51, 96, 112
Russia, 80

S

safety, 31, 71, 77, 100, 101
Sarajevo, 64, 73, 74, 79, 85, 87
savings, ix, 31, 37, 45, 48, 49, 53, 62, 71, 78, 80, 81, 83, 89, 99
scaling, 95
scope, x, 10, 12, 41, 53, 64, 89, 90, 94, 112
Secretary of Defense, 96, 98, 99, 100
security, viii, 2, 5, 8, 66, 71, 76, 78, 91
security services, 76
security threats, 66
Senate, vii, 1, 4, 8, 15, 20, 25, 54, 97, 99
Senate Committee on Environment and Public Works, vii, 1, 4
Serbia, 64, 85
service provider, 45
services, x, 23, 27, 32, 36, 37, 38, 44, 45, 89, 91, 92, 95, 112
shelter, 11
shoreline, 36
signs, 25
site cleanup, 33
social security, 15, 69, 112
Social Security Administration, 15, 112
social structure, 98
specialists, 42
specifications, 63, 99
spending, 7, 20, 24, 25, 44, 46, 49, 51, 54, 56, 67
spreadsheets, 13
St. Petersburg, 80
stability, 54, 56
staffing, 78, 79, 87
stakeholders, 43, 54
state(s), ix, x, 11, 12, 35, 36, 40, 47, 53, 54, 56, 74, 77, 81, 89, 90, 91, 92, 93, 94, 99, 102, 105, 107, 109, 110
state laws, 102
statutes, x, 90, 98, 102, 113
statutory authority, x, 89, 91, 94, 95
storage, 101
structure, 19, 21, 40, 41, 42, 43, 44, 45, 47, 53, 57, 91, 98, 99, 102
Superfund, 106, 115
surplus, 69, 86, 92, 93, 94, 97, 98, 100, 102, 103, 104, 105, 106, 107, 108, 109, 112, 114

T

tanks, 101
Tanzania, 66
target, 78
taxpayers, 20, 21, 42
technical comments, ix, 18, 53
technological developments, 95
technologies, 107, 108
telecommunications, 5
temporary housing, x, 89, 91
tenants, 55
Tennessee Valley Authority, 47

threats, 66, 98
time frame, 61, 70, 77, 78, 82
Title V, 93
total revenue, 54, 56
tracks, 9
trade, 5, 23
training, 95, 108
transactions, 22, 32, 35, 41, 69, 81, 104
transparency, ix, 11, 13, 18, 19, 21, 22, 28, 42, 98
transportation, 56, 71
Treasury, 15, 57, 112
treatment, 20
tribal officials, 110

U

U.S. Department of Agriculture, 18
U.S. Postal Service, x, 21, 90, 91, 95, 112, 113, 114
U.S. Treasury, 32
Ukraine, 77
United, v, 17, 20, 21, 59, 62, 64, 85, 87, 88, 97, 106, 107, 108, 109, 112
United Kingdom, 64, 85
United States, v, 17, 20, 21, 59, 62, 64, 87, 88, 97, 106, 107, 108, 109, 112
urban, 67
USDA, ix, 17, 18, 19, 21, 22, 27, 29, 30, 32, 35, 38, 53
USPS, x, 90, 91, 92, 94, 95, 96, 113, 115
Uzbekistan, 69

V

vegetation, 108
vessels, 99
violent crime, 46
Volunteers, 37, 38
vote, 114
vulnerability, 66

W

waiver, 65, 80, 81
Washington, 3, 6, 30, 34, 38, 54, 55, 56, 57, 86, 87, 88
waste, 54
water, 35, 56
wholesale, 98
wildlife, 112
wildlife conservation, 112
workers, 113
worldwide, ix, 60, 62, 70, 72, 77, 79, 83, 90